LITTLEJOHN'S
SOUTH CAROLINA
JUDICIAL HISTORY
1930 – 2004

BRUCE LITTLEJOHN

This book was made possible through the generous support of the South Carolina Bar Foundation.

DEDICATION

Dedicated to the many lawyers who educated me as a judge on circuit sufficiently to convince the General Assembly that I was entitled to a promotion.

– Bruce Littlejohn

THE JOGGLING BOARD

Legend has it that the idea for the joggling board came to South Carolina from Scotland in the early 1800s. The long board supported by rockers at each end allows two or more persons to rock together. This playful outdoor furniture became a common sight in the 19th century, gracing Southern porches, yards and piazzas. It was thought to be useful in easing rheumatism, aiding digestion and bolstering courtships. Some say that no daughter went unmarried in any Antebellum house that was host to a joggling board.

JogglingBoardpress

Published by Joggling Board Press
Joggling Board Press, LLC
P.O. Box 13029
Charleston, SC 29422
www.jogglingboardpress.com

Editor/Susan Kammeraad-Campbell
Jacket and text design/John Costa

First printing 2005
Printed in the United States.

A CIP catalog record for this book has been applied for from the U.S. Library of Congress.

ISBN 0-9753498-6-4

ABOUT THE AUTHOR

Cameron Bruce Littlejohn is an icon in South Carolina history. He has served his state and nation as:

- Premier South Carolina attorney
- Military leader during and after World War II, who served as a military prosecutor of Japanese war criminals
- Member of the S.C. House of Representatives
- Speaker, S.C. House of Representatives
- Distinguished S.C. Circuit Court judge, 17 years
- Associate justice, S.C. Supreme Court, 17 years
- Chief justice, S.C. Supreme Court, 1 ½ years
- Acting judge, S.C. Court of Appeals, 10 years

Chief Justice Littlejohn was born on July 22, 1913, in the small farming and mill community of Pacolet, in Spartanburg County, South Carolina, the youngest of eight children of Lady Sara Warmoth and Cameron Littlejohn. He graduated from Pacolet High School and from Wofford College in 1933. He attended and graduated from the University of South Carolina School of Law where he was a member of the debate team and president of the senior law class.

Upon graduation from law school in 1936, Littlejohn returned to Spartanburg to practice law, then stood for the S.C. House of Representatives and was elected. On February 7, 1942, he married Inell Smith of Inman. He served with distinction in the S.C. House for seven years, resigning on October 25, 1943, to volunteer as a private in the U.S. Army. He was discharged as a first lieutenant in 1946 after foreign service, which included a tour of duty in the Philippines as a military prosecutor of Japanese war criminals.

On February 9, 1949, Littlejohn was elected judge for the Seventh Judicial Circuit. As he rode the circuit, he soon came to be recognized as one of the state's most able, fair and popular trial judges. He presided

Chief Justice Bruce Littlejohn

over his court with dignity and firmness. His disarming wit, easy-going manner, warm personality and, especially, his patience with young lawyers made his visits to each circuit a welcomed event.

As a trial judge, this man managed to earn the respect and admiration of the attorneys who appeared before him, regardless of the outcome of their cases. His keen insight and distinguished demeanor on the trial bench were tempered with a sense of humor and charm, which endeared him to those around him. His book, *Laugh with the Judges,* published in 1974, is a delightful compendium of trial antidotes, which provides the reader with the opportunity to view the legal profession through the eyes of one of its shrewdest observers. Above all, a sense of legal genius and fairness pervaded Judge Littlejohn's courtroom.

As Justice Littlejohn, his gift for legal reasoning and proficient opinion writing swiftly became apparent. Whether his thoughts reflected what ultimately became the majority or the minority view, they were always met with the respect and careful consideration of his colleagues.

Judge Littlejohn's transition to chief justice was easily accomplished given his natural leadership qualities and the respect already accorded him by his brethren. He was at once a brilliant legal scholar and persuasive diplomat. His unique personality had well-prepared him for his position as administrative head of the unified judicial system, where he instilled a sense of cooperation and common purpose among the various courts. Moreover, he was an effective liaison between the judiciary and other branches of state government and was adept at resolving conflicts between them.

In retirement, Chief Justice Littlejohn continued to be active as a judge, serving as an acting judge for the S.C. Court of Appeals for more than 10 years.

Chief Justice Littlejohn's commitment to diversity was demonstrated when he used his authority to appoint acting supreme court justices to allow Carol Connor and Jasper Cureton to become, respectively, the first woman and the first African-American to serve on the state's highest court.

     – Jean H. Toal
     Chief Justice of the Supreme Court of South Carolina

PREVIOUS BOOKS BY
BRUCE LITTLEJOHN

Laugh with the Judge, 1974
Littlejohn's Half Century at the Bench and Bar, 1987
Littlejohn's Political Memoirs, 1934-1988, 1988

TABLE OF CONTENTS

INTRODUCTION

Why, one may fairly ask, another book? Why this book? I will allow our author to address this inquiry himself (as he must have anticipated such questions), which he does in his opening chapter. Of deep interest to me, however, is what our author does not set out to write about – himself. Autobiographies, he once commented to me, present a temptation and opportunity to embellish one's accomplishments and person. And so he writes instead, in his easygoing and straightforward style, about what most interests him – happenings in the South Carolina legal system over the course of his legal career since graduating from South Carolina Law School in 1936. (He still actively practices law today, having recently participated as co-counsel in a multi-million dollar class action lawsuit which settled.)

Yet behind the words, underlying the happenings described, emerges the man. It cannot be otherwise. Speaking of one's true character, Jesus said, "Out of the overflow of your heart, the mouth speaks." We speak in words, written or verbal, and in deeds. In her splendid book, *If You Want to Write*, Brenda Ueland applies this truism to writers: "The personality behind the writing is so important … On the paper there are all the neatly written words and sentences … But behind the words and sentences, there is this deep, moving thing – the personality of the writer. And whatever that personality is, it will shine through the writing and make it noble or greater, or touching or niggardly or supercilious or whatever the writer is. The personality of the writer will be revealed – by the nature of the subject matter, by the events and happenings recounted, and by the manner of description chosen."

Bruce Littlejohn writes about that which most interests him – the legal system – and especially the lawyers and judges ("bench and bar") in South Carolina. He typically chooses events and happenings reflecting change, not merely to reminisce but to reflect upon the dynamic nature of society and laws as well as the constant need to improve and modify the legal system to meet ever-increasing demands. He describes such matters usually as an eyewitness, because he was oftentimes at the forefront or at least in the middle of many such developments. Because of his personal involvement, his keen interest in the legal system, his astute insight into human nature and societal trends, and his uncanny ability to recount events, no one is more qualified than Judge Littlejohn to address such matters of historical interest. As for his own role, our author does not succumb to the temptation to embellish himself or his personal accomplishments, preferring instead to recognize the role of others and the collective good, the best that can be accomplished when people work together (judicial and legislative, bench and bar, lawyers and laypersons) in a non-confrontational, respectful manner toward a common goal for the common good.

Those who have had the privilege and, indeed, the pleasure of knowing Bruce Littlejohn know of his good humor, his fondness for good company, his intelligence, his convictions, his forward thinking and especially his humility. These have been his lifelong badges, as lawyer, legislator and judge. "Humility" derives from the Latin root humilis, meaning low, humble and humus, meaning ground or earth. It denotes an underlying recognition of one's role – significant and insignificant at the same time – in the grand scheme of things. It binds the man of accomplishments to the common man. A humble man remains grounded in his relationships with and understanding of people from all walks of life.

Our author was born July 22, 1913, in the rural community of Pacolet in Spartanburg County. He was the youngest of eight children. His father worked as a rural letter carrier and a farmer. Littlejohn was educated in the public schools of Pacolet, then at Wofford College and finally at the University of South Carolina School of Law. At age 23, he was elected to the S.C. House of Representatives where he served for seven years. As a state representative, he was deferred from the World War II draft, but waived the exemption and volunteered to serve in the U.S. Army. Upon his return from the war, he was again elected to the legislature and served as speaker from 1947-49. In 1949, he was made resident judge of the Seventh Judicial Circuit where he served for 17 years before being elevated to the Supreme Court of South Carolina.

After 17 years as a member of that court, he was elected chief justice, serving until mandatory retirement in 1985.

He has been the recipient of many honors: 1) Spartanburg Chamber of Commerce's Neville Holcombe Distinguished Public Service Award; 2) S.C. Bar Foundation's DuRant Distinguished Public Service Award; 3) Kiwanis' Man of the Year Award; 4) Rotary Club Paul Harris Award; 5) Honorary member of Phi Beta Kappa; and 6) Honorary doctorate degrees from Wofford College, Converse College, Limestone College and the University of South Carolina. In 2004, he was presented the state's highest civilian honor, the Order of the Palmetto. Simultaneously, Highway 176, which connects Pacolet where he was born and Spartanburg where he now resides, was named Bruce Littlejohn Boulevard. On this road, he will return to his roots, his home, his humble beginning – to be buried in Pacolet.

– Alan M. Tewkesbury Jr., Esquire
Friend, neighbor and former law clerk (1980-81)

FOREWORD

Why This Book?

In 1987, I published a book entitled *Littlejohn's Half Century at the Bench and Bar*. It was, in effect, my legal memoirs dating back to law school days beginning in 1933. The manuscript was donated to the South Carolina Bar Foundation, which published and marketed it. In 1989, I published a book entitled *Littlejohn's Political Memoirs*. It was in effect a recitation of my experiences and observations in South Carolina politics from 1934 to 1988. This one was donated to Wofford College.

I had hoped that someone would write the history of the South Carolina judiciary, but inasmuch as I found no one in the mood, I undertook the project myself. I feel at least minimally qualified to write such a book. I have been a party to, or at least intensely interested in, all of the changes that have taken place in the law and the judiciary since I began a career at the University of South Carolina Law School in the mid-1930s. These experiences include 13 years at the practice of law, three years as a prosecutor of Japanese war criminals during World War II, 10 years as a member of the S.C. House of Representatives during which I served as speaker for three years, 17 years as a circuit court judge, 17 years as an associate justice of the Supreme Court of South Carolina, 16 months as chief justice, and nine years after retirement holding court by special appointment. These experiences enabled me to call upon my memory for a great portion of this book.

In this undertaking, I have attempted to point out not only the personnel involved in the judicial system but also the changes in the work, which judges undertake. Every person who writes a book has a great temptation to make herself or himself a heroine or a hero on every page. In my previous writings, I resisted the temptation. I have tried again to resist the temptation, but it is inescapable that many personal references will, of necessity, be made. One of the purposes of the S.C. Bar Foundation is to record the history of the bench and bar. I submit this book as my effort to help the foundation accomplish this goal.

– Bruce Littlejohn

THE EARLY YEARS

1 As It Was in 1930

In 1930 and before, South Carolina was largely an agricultural state. The primary farm products of the day were cotton and tobacco. This was the beginning of the Great Depression resulting in part from the stock market collapsing in 1929. Businesses stagnated and unemployment was rampant. It was not until two years later, when Franklin Roosevelt was elected U.S. President, that we began to experience more prosperous times. When there is little activity, there is usually a minimum of court need. People litigate because they go places and do things and create problems.

At that time there were 14 judicial circuits. The constitution allowed the legislature to designate the judicial circuits – the fourteenth circuit having been created in 1919. Then as now, the fourteenth circuit is comprised of Allendale, Hampton, Jasper, Beaufort and Colleton counties. Holding any judicial office at that time was quite prestigious. The pay was not great, but it was commensurate with what lawyers were earning and what executives were paid. At that time, circuit court judges and members of the supreme court were paid about

$5,000 annually. The workload was modest with no courts of appeals or family courts. Divorces were prohibited by law until 1949.

The constitution permitted the legislature to create additional courts as needed with less jurisdiction than a circuit court and more jurisdiction than a magistrate's court. At that time, the magistrate could sentence one to pay up to a $100 fine or serve up to 30 days. He could handle a civil case involving not more than $100. All of the circuit court judges and members of the supreme court at that time were elected by a joint session of the S.C. House of Representatives and S.C. Senate. Many members of the bar and public questioned this method of selecting judges. The debate continues to this day. Many people think there ought to be a better way to elect judges. I am inclined to agree with the opinion of Judge Loomis in his book, *The Trial Judge*: "There is no good way to elect judges; certainly there is no perfect way to elect judges. Any system used will give you some good ones, some sorry ones and a whole lot in between. If the method being used is producing reasonably good judges, that system should be continued." It is not contemplated that the legislature will, in the foreseeable future, give up the authority to elect judges.

Being a member of the court in the 1930s was truly a Southern gentleman's undertaking. Judges were only partially employed. Even as late as 1967, the supreme court was handling only 151 appeals annually. That figure today is approximately 1,000 cases every year.

Circuit court judges were constitutionally required to rotate among the circuits, a system designated by the legislature. The general assembly undertook to tell all 14 circuit court judges where they would hold court any given Monday. I thought it was a stupid system; no one was giving thought to sending the judicial power where it was most needed. By this time judges were, in large measure, driving motor vehicles to court on dirt roads as well as paved roads. Some of the judges were traveling to their assignments by train.

In 1930, the Supreme Court of South Carolina was composed of Chief Justice Eugene Blease, and Associate Justices Thomas Cothran, John Stabler, Jesse Carter and Milledge Bonham. Blease was the brother of Cole Blease who had formerly served as governor and, from 1924 to 1930, was a member of the U.S. Senate. Traditionally, a senior associate justice had been elevated to the office of chief justice, but Eugene Blease ran out of turn and was elected. He served only a short time, resigning October 8, 1934, and returning to Newberry where he practiced law for approximately 30 years before his death. Rumor held he was unpopular with the associate justices because he had run out of turn and decided to leave the court rather than experience their ire.

In those days, there were approximately 800 lawyers in South Carolina. Today, there are approximately 12,000, but only about 9,000 are engaged in daily activities at the bar. Many of the lawyers and judges were graduates of the University of South Carolina School of Law or some other school of law. A portion of them, however, came to be lawyers, as permitted under court rules, by standing the state bar examination after having read law for two years in the office of some South Carolina attorney. It was not until 1952 that this system of qualifying to stand the examination was abolished.

Among those who studied in a lawyer's office for two years before standing the law examination were J. Strom Thurmond and James F. Byrnes. At that time, and until the early 1950s, the supreme court honored what we refer to as the "diploma privilege." One who was a graduate of an accredited law school in another state could be admitted to the practice by merely showing his or her diploma. At that time and until the late 1970s, the state recognized what we refer to as the "rule of comity." If one practiced law in another state for a period of three or five years, such a one could automatically be admitted here without standing for the bar exam. The comity system was abolished because the court found that South Carolina was getting a lot of substandard lawyers. A lawyer who was in trouble in Texas or Tennessee or some other state would seek a new place to set up shop. Today, if a lawyer from another state wants to practice law in South Carolina, he or she must stand for the state bar examination.

By reason of the automatic rotation system, circuit judges could tell where they would be sent any given Monday several years hence. For example, the legislature might say there would be two weeks of common pleas court in Aiken on the first Monday of January whether there was any business to be conducted or not. This was a tremendous waste of judge power in my estimation.

In the early 1930s, the resident circuit court judges were as follows:

First Circuit	M.M. Mann
Second Circuit	Hayne Rice
Third Circuit	Phillip Stoll

Fourth Circuit	E.C. Dennis
Fifth Circuit	W.H. Townsend
Sixth Circuit	A.L. Gaston
Seventh Circuit	Thomas S. Sease
Eighth Circuit	C.C. Featherstone
Ninth Circuit	W.H. Grimball
Tenth Circuit	G.B. Green
Eleventh Circuit	C.J. Ramage
Twelfth Circuit	S.W. Shipp
Thirteenth Circuit	Dewey Oxner
Fourteenth Circuit	Henry Johnson

Because of the inefficiency of the circuit court rotation system, the legislature created several county courts in the larger counties. These courts had more jurisdiction than a magistrate but less than a circuit court judge. All of these county courts exercised such different jurisdiction as the legislature designated.

2 Criminal Practices in Early Days

Circuit court judges, as far back as I can remember, held court in large measure as court was held in England. It has been said that some of the customs adhered to in our courts were brought over on the *Mayflower* and that no great change was made until the last half of the twentieth century. Under the rotation system, judges held court in an assigned circuit in January, February, March and April. Every resident circuit judge came home to his own circuit and held such court as was needed in May, June, July and August of every year. The other months of the year, September, October, November and December, judges held court in another assigned circuit.

Their criminal courts were conducted in a manner quite different from that of trials today. Murder, rape and attempted rape were capital offenses until the Supreme Court of the United States held that sentences for execution for rape or attempted rape were unconstitutional. The supreme court rationalized that such was cruel and unusual, as well as a violation of the Eighth Amendment of the U.S. Constitution. Today, murder is the only capital offense.

The judges tried capital cases in the same manner as other cases. *Voir dire* consisted of three simple questions prior to beginning a capital case. Judges asked the jurors: "Are you opposed to capital punishment?" then "Are you related by blood or marriage to the defendant?" and then "Are you related by blood or marriage to the victim?" If these questions were answered satisfactorily to the judge, the juror was seated. At that time, only men served on the jury. Statutory law said that juries would be composed of men. It was not until 1967, when the Supreme Court of the United States held that juries must be drawn from a representative group of the populace, that women first sat on juries. Women had been sitting on juries in other courts throughout the country before that time.

Until about 1962, sentences of execution would be appealed to the Supreme Court of South Carolina and, if the verdict were affirmed, the defendant would be executed promptly – usually within six months. All of this changed when the Supreme Court of the United States began rewriting the rules of criminal procedure which had to be adhered to by all the state courts. The Supreme Court of the United States prior thereto ruled that a murder case did not involve any federal issue. It consistently ruled that a criminal case involving a capital sentence was a matter purely for the state courts.

In a capital case today, one or two weeks are often required to qualify a jury. It is difficult for my young friends to believe that I tried a capital case on a Thursday and sentenced the defendant to execution following a guilty verdict by the jury. On the following day, I tried another capital case and sentenced that defendant to execution after the jury verdict. Both cases were appealed to the supreme court and affirmed, and the defendants were then promptly executed.

3 Judges' Retirement

During the first half of the twentieth century, retirement systems for any government and/or private employees were few and far between. Supreme Court of South Carolina and S.C. Circuit Court judges were no exception. Social Security did not come into being until the mid-1930s. Further, pay for judges during this era was not great. Certainly it was not sufficient to permit a judge to accumulate enough assets to retire in comfort.

Prior to the retirement system coming into being in 1945, judges held on to their offices oftentimes years after they were capable of serving. The legislature hesitated to oust a judge for reelection and often a disabled judge would have to impose upon other members of the court to carry out his portion of the work. The story is told of one member of the supreme court who was truly disabled but was up for reelection. To make it appear that he was still capable of work, his friends hauled him to Columbia to sit on the supreme court so as to give the appearance of capability. It is said that pictures were being reviewed and, when they were handed to this judge, he looked at them upside down.

The time came in 1945 when the general assembly determined to do something about the situation. It enacted the judges' retirement system whereby a judge was required to retire at age 72, whether incapacitated or not. Some of the judges nearing retirement age lobbied against this provision but without success. Under the terms of the retirement law, a member of the supreme court or a member of the circuit court drew retirement during the remainder of his life equaling approximately 70 percent of his regular pay. Widows of retired judges were allowed to draw one-third of the amount which her husband would have drawn were he still living. At the time of the passage of the retirement law, members of the courts were still only about half-employed. The assignments were still highly desirable even with or without the retirement law.

It is my observation that the work of the judges now has become so burdensome that a large portion of the members of the courts are retiring just as soon as they become eligible. The law provided that a retired judge was subject to call but did not have to serve unless he so desired. By reason of this provision, quite a few of the judges have taken special assignments at the direction of the chief justice over the years. In the mid-1990s, the legislature passed a law requiring retired judges be screened before they could accept assignments. For all practical purposes, this cut off the supply because only a few judges in retirement have agreed to be screened.

Prior to about 1975, the 16 solicitors serving the 16 judicial circuits were permitted to practice law. In most circuits, the work of a solicitor was not demanding. In other circuits, the solicitor never got caught up with the docket. The time had come when the legislature wanted to require all solicitors to work full time. The solicitors formed a powerful lobby to influence the legislature to reject this requirement. The legislature compromised on the issue with the solicitors by agreeing for them to be placed under the judges' retirement system so that today a solicitor enjoys the same retirement benefits as a member of the supreme court or circuit court. Certainly, the time has now come when the prosecutions of criminal cases in the court of general sessions is such that no solicitor would have time to practice law on the side. Today, each solicitor has quite a few assistant solicitors and investigators. Few solicitors are able to keep current with the dockets. The retirement system has enticed many competent lawyers to seek judgeships, a station they might not otherwise pursue.

4 The New Supreme Court Building of 1971*

When the S.C. State House was built, space was provided on the second floor for meetings of the senate and the house of representatives. Small committee rooms and the engrossing department, which is now known as the legislative council, were included on the same floor. The offices of the governor, the supreme court, the state treasurer, the comptroller general and the secretary of state were on the ground floor. When I came to the law in 1936, space for all of these was considered reasonably adequate.

The supreme court quarters consisted of the courtroom, the clerk's office, the library and the conference room. These consumed approximately 1,400 square feet of floor space. The justices had no offices; all five used the conference room as headquarters. The conference room, which adjoined the library, was across the hall from the courtroom. Prior to hearings, the justices assembled in the conference room and were robed. They then paraded across the hall, sometimes meandering through spectators and visitors who were taking a tour of the capitol building. The permanent staff of the court consisted of the clerk and some three or four other employees.

The work of the court at that time was not burdensome. As late as 1967, when I became a member, only 151 appeals were filed during the entire 12-month period. The space occupied by the court was on the east end of the State House, where the lieutenant governor and others now maintain office space. At that time the house and senate members had no offices. The Blatt, Brown, Gressette and Dennis buildings had not yet been constructed.

Under the administration of Governor Fritz Hollings, the offices of the governor were moved from the state house to the Wade Hampton Office Building. When Governor Robert McNair was elevated to the governor's office after the appointment of Governor Donald Russell to the U.S. Senate in 1965, plans were made to return the governor's office to the state house. In order to accommodate this move, the offices of the state treasurer, the comptroller general and the secretary of state were moved to the Wade Hampton Office Building in 1966.

During my years at the bar, the need for additional governmental office space grew tremendously. It was apparent that the legislature, which needed more room, was eyeballing the space occupied by the Supreme Court of South Carolina. It was feasible for the supreme court to be relocated, but its members were not very cooperative. Among those opposed to giving up space in the state house were Chief Justices D. Gordon Baker and later Claude A. Taylor. They simply liked the idea of remaining close to the house and senate.

Across the street from the state house, at the corner of Sumter and Gervais streets, was the Columbia Post Office. Built in September 1921, the building was occupied as a post office until the mid-1960s when a new post office was constructed and occupied on Assembly Street. *The Columbia Record* of March 8, 1963, carried a story which read in part as follows: "The Senate set in motion today a proposal to take over the soon-to-be-abandoned Columbia Post Office for use by the Supreme Court of South Carolina. The Senate passed and sent to the House a resolution that would establish a committee to look into the feasibility of acquiring the federal property. The building is located on Gervais and Sumter streets directly across from the State House grounds. The Supreme Court chambers are now in the State House."

When Chief Justice Taylor died in January 1966, Joseph R. Moss succeeded him as chief justice. Robert E. McNair was then governor. Each took a different view about moving the court out of the state house. In a letter from the chief justice to the governor, he writes, "It has come to the attention of the supreme court that there is a strong possibility that the state may be able to acquire the site of the old Columbia Post Office building through general services of the federal government. The supreme court is not only aware of its need for additional space, but is cognizant of the fact that the office of the governor, when returned to the state house, and the general assembly will be handicapped because of limited space. Since the Columbia Post Office fits closely in the state government complex, the supreme court today unanimously agreed that a request should be directed to you asking that the Columbia Post Office building be acquired by the state and designated solely for the use of the Supreme Court." This request followed an informal discussion with the Honorable Edgar A. Brown, member of the S.C. Budget and Control Board.

In the meantime, the City of Columbia acquired the old post office property. In 1968, the state took title from the city with the view of converting the building into quarters for the Supreme Court of South Carolina. The purchase price was $750,000. While it would be difficult to make most post office buildings look like a courthouse, this one, with its with large columns and grand architectural design, was the exception. When the building was converted, it was only necessary to remove the words "United States Post Office" and replace them with "The Supreme Court of South Carolina." On the other hand, much needed to be done inside the building to convert it to court needs. A post office normally has inside a great deal of work space with extremely high ceilings. I think it would be a fair appraisal to say that the architects and contractors literally gutted the building's interior and started over.

A wall of postal boxes and service windows separated the main lobby of the post office from the tremendous mailroom that soared from the ground floor to the rooftop. Today the first floor includes the courtroom, with specially designed wall coverings and custom-made carpeting. In addition, each justice has an office, along with space for the clerk of court offices. On the second floor is the library, a two-level arrangement with stock space for an eventual 80,000 volumes, as well as a small courtroom housing the original bench from the state house. A mezzanine has been converted to a gallery, which displays portraits and other artifacts. Offices for staff attorneys are also on the second floor. The lower level of the supreme court building provides additional office and storage space for the clerk of court.

Frances Smith, clerk of court from 1959 to 1983, acted as liaison with architects, contractors and designers. She deserves much credit for the planning and completion of the supreme court building, of which the state can be proud.

The court moved into its new quarters in January 1971. Serving on the court with me at that time were Chief Justice Joseph R. Moss and Associate Justices J. Woodrow Lewis, Thomas P. Bussey and James M. Brailsford Jr. Prior to the ratification of the Unified Court System Amendment to the Constitution in 1973, comparatively little staff was needed by the court, which at that time was hearing an average of 200 cases per year.

The needs of the court changed considerably after 1973. New Article V of the South Carolina Constitution made the chief justice the administrative head of the entire unified court system. Prior to that time, the legislature had pretty well operated the court system by statute. In South Carolina, we had a hodgepodge of courts and no accountability. As the chief justice assumed the duty of operating the court system, the need for staff members multiplied – so much so that today the office of court administrator must be quartered at another location.

The appellate courts now dispose of about 1,000 cases every year.

*Adapted from *Littlejohn's Half Century at the Bench and Bar (1936–1986)*.

5 Courthouse and Courtroom Facilities

The courthouses of today compared with the courthouses of the 1930s are substantially different. The courthouses of yesterday did not provide office space for the circuit court judges, so they operated out of their residences. If a lawyer needed to get an order signed, he simply went to the judge's home. Today, county government is required to provide office space. Not until the early 1990s were circuit court judges provided with secretarial help. Until then, the judges asked their court reporters or imposed on lawyers' secretaries for the writing of orders and correspondence.

Persons walked freely in and out of the courthouse without being required to subject themselves to metal detectors. About 1960, a county court judge hearing a domestic matter in Bennettsville ruled against the husband in a child custody case. The ruling was in open court and raised the ire of the husband who took a pistol from his belt and killed the judge. Some years later a defendant who had been out on bond in

Spartanburg walked in off the streets to stand trial. Upon being found guilty, he was taken by the sheriff to the adjoining county jail. En route he took a pistol from his belt and began shooting. Fortunately, no one was hurt or killed, but several motor vehicles were damaged. Recent national events, such as 911, have caused most, if not all, courthouse custodians to study the matter of security to protect the judges and court personnel.

Since World War II, most of the counties have either built new courthouses or brought about major renovations so that today courthouse and courtroom facilities are fairly adequate. Gone are the days when a courtroom was heated with a potbellied stove and sometimes a fireplace. Gone are the oscillating fans that helped to cool the courtroom. All courthouses today are air conditioned and provided with central heating facilities. Gone also – with one or two rare exceptions – is the dock. Until recently, courtroom architects thought they had to put the judge's bench in the middle of the courtroom. With rare exception, the judge's bench is now placed in the corner. This gives lawyers and witnesses work space not available under the old system.

The work of the court reporter also has changed. Years ago, practically all court reporters were men. There was a feeling that womenfolk should not be subjected to all the bad talk that went on in rape cases and other felonies. A court reporter only needed a pencil and a steno pad. Today a court reporter must record everything by stenotype and must have a back-up system in the form of a recorder.

Not until 1967 were women permitted to decorate the jury box. Until that year the code mandated that juries be composed of men. Women were permitted to practice law in South Carolina after 1918 by reason of statute, but it was not until the 1960s that women began to frequent the courtrooms of all courts.

6 Oath of Office

From the adoption of the Constitution of 1895 until the year 1955, judges and others required to take an oath of office had to swear that they had not engaged in a duel as principal, second or otherwise since 1881. I took such an oath of office 11 times, each time swearing that I had not engaged in a duel since 32 years before I was born. And I had to swear I would not, during the term of office to which I had been elected, engage in a duel as principal, second or otherwise. On six occasions – when I entered upon the office as a member of the S.C. House of Representatives, twice as speaker, two times as a circuit court judge and once as a notary public – I had to take such an oath of office.

Before the turn of the century, it was not unusual for persons whose honor had been called into question to challenge to duel the person alleged to have inflicted the insult. Those who did not accept the challenge were considered cowards. Perhaps the inspiration for including the requirement in the Constitution of 1895 came from the well-publicized Cash–Shannon duel of 1880. In that duel, fought near Camden, Col. E.B.C. Cash, who was the father-in-law of Judge Richard Cannon Watts, killed a lawyer named Col. William M. Shannon with the first bullet fired. Cash was tried for murder to a mistrial and retried to an acquittal. If one challenged a public office holder to a duel, he was placed in an awkward position. The constitutional provision was included so as to give public office holders an acceptable reason for not responding to the challenge.

The part that dueling played in American political life and in American society is illustrated by the famous duel between Alexander Hamilton and Aaron Burr in 1805. Hamilton had exerted great influence against Burr in favor of Thomas Jefferson in the presidential election and had opposed Burr in his candidacy for governor of New York. Burr forced a quarrel and challenged Hamilton to a duel. Although he strongly disapproved of dueling, Hamilton felt obliged to meet the challenge. They dueled in New Jersey; Hamilton was mortally wounded and died the next day.

The oath was required under the Constitution of South Carolina until 1955 when it was amended to eliminate the requirement. At a general election in 1954, the public voted in the change. The amendment was ratified in the spring of 1955 and, accordingly, office holders now may engage in duels if they so choose without violating their oath of office. The requirement was not totally without reason and finds more justification in history than would appear at first blush.

Just in case any member of the bench or bar is tempted to duel, I call attention to §16-3-430 of the 1976 Code. It reads in part: "…in case any person shall kill another in a duel with a deadly weapon … such person so killing another … shall suffer death, as in the case of willful murder." Historically, persons who killed another while fighting a duel were tried for murder but were usually exonerated. Officers are now required to take an oath of office less complicated and more logical as follows: "I do solemnly swear (or affirm) that I am duly qualified, according to the Constitution of this State, to exercise the duties of the office to which I have been elected (or appointed), and that I will to the best of my ability, discharge the duties thereof, and preserve, protect, and defend the Constitution of this State and of the United States. So help me God." In addition, judges and lawyers are now required to take a special oath prepared by the supreme court.

7 The Dock*

Judges and lawyers are defenders of the status quo. It is easier to keep on doing something the same way than to figure out a better procedure. Often lawyers have attempted to defend their views by saying, "Judge, that's the way we have always done it." This is a very poor reason.

Early in my career as a trial judge, I became interested in the use of the dock in the trial of criminal cases. Many of my young lawyer friends are completely unaware of the definition of a dock or its purpose. For them I quote the *Black's Law Dictionary* definition of a dock as follows: "The cage or enclosed space in a criminal court where prisoners stand when brought in for trial." The Massachusetts Supreme Judicial Court has described the dock as follows: "Most court rooms used for criminal sessions in the Commonwealth are equipped with a dock, a wooden enclosure, usually measuring four or five feet square, in which it has long been customary for the defendant to sit during trial. The dock is open at the top, so that the upper torso of a seated person is visible. The judge, the court clerk, court officers and the jury occupy similar enclosures, the arrangement of which varies from court room to court room. The dock as we know it appears to be a vestige of the English bale-dock."

My research of the South Carolina Constitution, the statutes and the rules of court revealed only one reference to the use of the dock. Rule 35 of the former Circuit Court Practice Rules included the following sentence: "No person shall be tried on an indictment unless personally present, except for misdemeanor; and upon the trial of any person charged with an offense for which the law requires that he should be arraigned, the Prisoner shall be placed in the dock."

I further learned that the dock was an idea brought over on the *Mayflower* from England. In England until this day, a person accused in a criminal case sits in the dock throughout the trial, several feet away from his attorney, so that discussions between the two are not possible. I concluded that this old-fashioned arrangement simply was not necessary in the conduct of a trial. It never occurred to me that the use of the dock might one day be challenged as being unconstitutional – I just thought it was stupid.

Within the courtroom where I presided for my first eight years as a circuit judge in Spartanburg, there was a conventional dock. It was often used, though not always, for the purpose of arraignment of defendants, especially those accused of murder. I do not recall, however, any prisoner in Spartanburg sitting in the dock throughout the trial of a case. I do recall one case where the defendant sat through the trial in the dock. That was in Charleston, where a defendant named Clisby was charged with rape. No mention was made relative to his occupying the dock seat. I sometimes wondered what effect, if any, his remaining in the dock had on the jury.

In some states, such as Massachusetts, use of the dock continues. In South Carolina, I find no issue having been raised relative to the use of the dock. In Massachusetts, however, a prisoner seeking post-conviction relief submitted to the court that his constitutional rights were violated when he was required to be seated in the dock during a trial. It contended that sitting in the dock during the trial was demeaning in the same way that wearing prison garb or handcuffs would be. In one case, the U.S. First Circuit Court of Appeals commented that "because confinement in the prison dock is unnecessary to accomplish any important state interest and may well dilute the presumption of innocence, the Massachusetts prisoner dock must be considered, as a general matter, to be an unconstitutional practice." The court, however, declined to grant relief on this basis but granted the relief sought on other grounds.

When a new courthouse was built to serve Richland County at the corner of Washington and Sumter streets in Columbia a half-century ago, Circuit Court Judge Duncan Bellinger was afraid not to provide a dock in the courtroom. At the same time, he did not think much of the idea. A compromise was reached – a portable dock. So far as I know, the portable dock they agreed upon and had built is the only one of its kind ever used in South Carolina. It was placed on rollers and stood at the back of the courtroom while civil court was in session. When criminal court was held, this dock was rolled within the bar and used in the conventional fashion.

I would estimate that there are probably five or six of the 46 county courthouses that still have a dock of some sort. As new courthouses are built and as major renovations take place in the older courthouses, they are eliminated altogether. When the plans were made for the new Spartanburg County Courthouse, dedicated in 1958, I instructed the planners to eliminate the dock.

It was with much glee that I proposed, in January of 1984, that reference to the dock be eliminated from Rule 35. The proposal was accepted and, accordingly, the dock in South Carolina is now history. The bailiffs' rod and staff also have gone the way of the dock. For several years when I first served as a trial judge, some of the courtroom bailiffs in a few counties were armed with a pole similar to a broom handle, about seven feet long. In case of any laughter or other disturbance, the bailiff would demand restoration of order by striking the staff against the floor. The court in Cherokee County was the last to abandon its use.

*Adapted from *Littlejohn's Half Century at the Bench and Bar (1936–1986).*

8 Changes in Criminal Procedure

It has been said that the Supreme Court of the United States is by degrees rewriting the rules of criminal procedure for all of the state courts. Three cases have brought about many procedural changes that control the way state trial judges conduct their work in the Court of General Sessions. In *Gideon v. Wainwright*, the Supreme Court of the United States ruled that in every serious case an accused person was entitled to an attorney, and if he could not afford one it was the duty of the trial judge to appoint one. *Arizona v. Miranda* held that confessions could not be taken unless the accused was given what we now refer to as his Miranda rights. *Illinois v. Escobedo* held that every person arrested was entitled to consult his lawyer as soon as the police investigation made him a prime suspect.

The necessity of appointing attorneys to represent accused persons slowed the work of the trial judge in criminal court. At first there was an effort on the part of many of the courts to appoint members of the bar to represent accused persons without any fee. It was said that the rendering of such a service was the price a lawyer pays for the privilege of practicing. This proved most unsatisfactory because many of the attorneys appointed had few skills and no experience in criminal court. The time came when it was decided that a better way to handle this problem was to set up a department of public defenders. Most of the public defenders are fulltime employees who supply representation to those who need an attorney and can't afford one. This arrangement brought about much plea bargaining.

It was widely thought that when the issue of plea bargaining came to be heard before the Supreme Court of the United States it would be outlawed. This, however, did not happen. The court smiled upon the thought that it would be tremendously helpful in clearing up congested dockets. The solicitor and public defender continued to plea bargain even if it involved giving away the courthouse for the sake of the docket. Ideally, there should be no plea bargaining. Plea bargaining has a tendency to shift the authority away from the judge to the solicitor when it comes to determining how much time a defendant serves. While a judge is not required to honor a plea bargain, as a practical matter he does so in nearly all cases. It is ironic that the government, which is prosecuting an accused person, pays the solicitor to secure a conviction and simultaneously pays a public defender to attempt to prevent one.

In days of yore, it was not unusual for a trial judge to accept 30 guilty pleas and impose 30 sentences in one day. More recently a judge must be convinced that a defendant understands all of the rights that he is giving up when he enters a guilty plea. Such explanation usually takes about 20 to 25 minutes for each individual pleading guilty. This makes it difficult for the judge to process more than 10 to 15 guilty pleas in a day. If the judge does not follow proper procedure, the accused person can raise the issue at a post-conviction hearing and may prevail.

Upon making an arrest, police officers now usually read the arrested person his Miranda Rights, which are as follows:

    1.   You have the right to remain silent.

2. Anything you say can and will be used against you in a court of law.
3. You have the right to talk to a lawyer and have him present with you while you are being questioned.
4. If you cannot afford to hire a lawyer, one will be appointed to represent you before any questioning, if you wish.

In 1986, the Supreme Court of the United States made two additional rulings, making it difficult to convict in capital punishment cases. It held that peremptory challenges, heretofore allowed without limitation to the government and the defendant, would now be subject to scrutiny and that jurors cannot be excused by the state because of their race. Now defense counsel may question the solicitor, requiring him to explain his reasons for excusing a juror. If the solicitor doesn't have a good reason, independent of race, the judge may seat the juror and deny the solicitor the right to use a peremptory challenge. In 1986, the court also ruled that a new trial must be held on the penalty phase of a trial when evidence was excluded from the trial relative to how an accused person acted in jail while awaiting trial in a capital punishment case. In effect, it held that whether or not the guilty person would make a good prisoner was relevant to the final sentence. Rule-making by the Supreme Court of the United States comes slowly and piecemeal. It must await an appropriate vehicle (or case) to give vent to the rule it would promulgate. Some may say the court promulgates rules through the back door and that this is a very poor vehicle for rule making.

9 Circuit Courts

Many portions of the South Carolina Constitution of 1895 are still in effect. That constitution provided that the state be divided into judicial circuits, and the legislature would have the authority to designate those counties which formed the respective circuits. The fourteenth circuit was created in 1919 and consisted of Hampton, Jasper, Beaufort, Colleton and Allendale counties. No additional circuits were formed until 1962.

It developed that the twelfth circuit, consisting of Florence, Marion, Georgetown and Horry counties, was overloaded. In 1962, the legislature created the fifteenth judicial circuit, leaving Florence and Marion counties as the twelfth circuit and designating Horry and Georgetown counties as the fifteenth circuit. Senator James B. Morrison was elected the first judge of the new fifteenth circuit. It also developed that there was more judicial work to be performed in the sixth and seventh circuits than could be handled by one resident judge. In 1966, the legislature created the sixteenth circuit, removing Union County from the seventh circuit and York County from the sixth circuit. Senator Robert Hayes was elected and served as the first resident judge of the newly created sixteenth circuit.

Recently, there has been little inclination to create new circuits. Instead, the legislature has been creating new judgeships so that today there are a total of 46 circuit court judges. There are two resident circuit court judges in the first, third, fourth, seventh, eighth, tenth, eleventh, fourteenth, fifteenth and sixteenth circuits. In the fifth, ninth and thirteenth circuits there are three resident judges. In addition there are, as of 2004, a total of 13 judges at large. These, as the name indicates, may be residents of any one of the 46 counties. All of the 46 circuit court judges are by constitutional directive required to rotate. Prior to 1973, automatic rotation was required by statute so that within a period of seven years each circuit court judge held court in all 46 counties. This rotation is now no longer automatic. Rotation is required, but the chief justice is permitted to rotate more or less systematically. For judges to rotate into counties distant from their residence is not always convenient, but the benefits of rotation offset such inconveniences.

Circuit courts have always been divided into two facets of judicial work – the court of general sessions having unlimited jurisdiction in criminal matters and the court of common pleas having general jurisdiction in all civil matters. Circuit court judges are elected for a term of six years at a joint session of the house and senate. They are permitted reelection until the end of the year of their 72nd birthday, when they must retire.

Within each of the circuits there is one solicitor. He or she is elected in the general election and may be reelected. The increase in the workload of the criminal courts is emphasized by the fact that until about 1960 solicitors did not have an assistant. The solicitor was permitted to practice law, and serving as solicitor was considered a part-time job. This changed about 1970 when the legislature passed an act making the office of solicitor a full-time job. Today, some solicitors have as many as 30 assistants. Being an assistant to a solicitor is a good way for young lawyers to get a lot of courtroom experience in a comparatively short period of time.

When I began holding court in 1950, each judicial circuit had one court reporter. They were all men except one. The thinking at that time seemed to be that women simply should not hear all of the ugly talk that went on in and about the courts. Today, there are nearly 100 court reporters assigned by the chief justice to the circuit and family courts. Nearly all are women.

Law clerks are now provided for each of the S.C. Circuit Court judges. Clerks traditionally serve for a period of one year, but a few make a career of it. A clerkship with either the S.C. Circuit Court, the S.C. Court of Appeals or the Supreme Court of South Carolina is a good substitute for an internship. A clerkship supplements such legal education as was received in law school. Some of the best young trial lawyers in the state learned the tricks of the trade while serving either as a law clerk or staff attorney.

10 Judges' Work in Capital Cases

Until about 1960, circuit court judges in South Carolina tried capital punishment cases like any other criminal case. At that time the death penalty could be imposed for rape, attempted rape or malicious murder. *Voir dire* questions to jurors were brief and the judge asked all of the questions. It was not unusual for a death penalty case to be tried in a day. Death penalty cases were routinely appealed to the Supreme Court of South Carolina. If the conviction was affirmed, execution would be carried out in approximately six months. Until 1962, the Supreme Court of the United States refused to take jurisdiction where state law only was involved. Until that time, it held there was no federal issue involved. But in 1962, the Supreme Court of the United States changed its mind and rationalized that there were two federal issues involved – the Sixth Amendment, guaranteeing a fair trial, and the Fourteenth Amendment, assuring due process.

Prior to this time, circuit court judges in the state were taking guilty pleas after basically asking a defendant if he committed the act. Judges took the word of the accused person when he said that he was guilty. This permitted circuit judges to accept guilty pleas and impose sentences in a comparatively short time. During a week of general sessions court, Monday and Tuesday were usually set aside for the taking of guilty pleas. Often a court reporter would not show up on those days because no record of the procedure was required.

It was about that time in the case of *Gideon v. Wainwright* that the the Supreme Court of the United States held that, in a criminal case, since a rich man could afford a lawyer, the government had to appoint a lawyer to represent a poor man. It is understandable that processing a case where a lawyer is involved takes considerably more time than a case in which the defendant has no attorney.

The Supreme Court of the United States further held that the states must provide a forum wherein an imprisoned person can contest the legality of his incarceration. Because of this requirement, legislatures throughout the country, including South Carolina, enacted a statute providing for what we now know as post-conviction relief hearings. Until then, it was the thinking in judicial and legal circles that one who was sentenced to prison gave up all rights. But then, the Supreme Court of the United States began holding that prisoners have substantial rights; substantial rights require judicial action and court proceedings. Now it is the case that prison authorities must provide prisoners a chapel in which to worship and a library to use in preparation for an application for post-conviction relief.

These protections were meant to ensure that an innocent person is not convicted. In an article I wrote for the S.C. Bar publication in 1985, I recited the protections provided to one accused of a crime. They are as follows:

> "1. The defendant may ask for a preliminary hearing; and if the Magistrate finds that there is no probable cause, the case will be dismissed.
>
> But if he does not:
>
> 2. The Solicitor upon receipt of the warrant can *nol pros* the case.
>
> But if he does not:
>
> 3. The Grand Jury may return a no bill.
>
> But if it does not:
>
> 4. The trial judge may, at the trial stage, grant a directed verdict.
>
> But if he does not:
>
> 5. The jury may refuse to convict if only one member votes "NO."
>
> But if it does not:

6. The trial judge may set the verdict aside.
   But if he does not:
7. The defendant may appeal to the State Supreme Court which may end the case or grant a new trial.
   But if it does not:
8. The defendant may petition the United States Supreme Court for a writ of *certiorari*, and that court may grant relief.
   But if it does not:
9. The defendant may bring a post-conviction relief action, and the state trial judge may grant relief.
   But if he does not:
10. The defendant may appeal to the State Supreme Court which may order post-conviction relief.
    But if it does not:
11. The defendant may petition for writ of *certiorari* in the United States Supreme Court which may grant relief.
    But if it does not:
12. The defendant may apply to a Federal District Court judge for post-conviction relief and that court may grant the petition.
    But if it does not:
13. The defendant may appeal to the United States Circuit Court of Appeals in Richmond, which may grant the petition.
    But if it does not:
14. The defendant may appeal to the United States Supreme Court which may grant relief."

And then there is, of course, always the possibility of rehashing a case because of evidence discovered after trial and/or because an important witness has recanted. Application for relief based on these two grounds tries the soul of a judge. I know because I have been there. New trials based on recantations may sometimes be appropriate, but will, generally, be looked upon by the courts with suspicion.

In order for the government to prevail and in order for the defendant to be punished, prosecuting authorities must prevail at all of these 14 stages. If the defendant prevails at any one of these stages, he may be freed, granted a new trial or given some other appropriate relief.

The bench and bar can be none too proud of the fact that justice may be so long delayed. The result is that as of 2004, there are more than 3,400 persons on death row throughout the United States. In South Carolina there are more than 70. In several instances attorneys have attempted to get the Supreme Court of the United States to abolish capital punishment. The court has refused to do so but has made it difficult to try a case to the court's satisfaction. Eventually, that court may change its mind again and rule "no more executions."

11 The Judges Ride Circuit*

The Constitution of 1895, under which the judicial system operated until the revised constitutional amendment of 1973, provided that the state would be divided into judicial circuits. It said that there would be one resident circuit judge for each circuit. The S.C. Legislature had authority to determine the circuits. As I came to the bench in 1949, there were 14 circuits composed of two, three, four or five counties, each depending on population. The 14 circuit court judges were elected at a joint meeting of members of the S.C. House of Representatives and the S.C. Senate, and this was the electing authority that made me a circuit judge in 1949. Members of the circuit court were elected for a four-year term. I was reelected in 1953, 1957, 1961 and 1965.

The constitution also provided that judges would be rotated and hold court in all counties. Under our system of rotation, each of the 14 circuit judges held court in his home circuit during the months of May, June, July and August. Each was assigned to other circuits during the remaining eight months of the year, and so, after leaving the second circuit where my judicial career began, I came home to preside over the 1950 terms of court for the summer in Spartanburg, Gaffney and Union. These three towns were the county seats of Spartanburg County, Cherokee County and Union County, respectively.

In actuality, circuit judges did not engage in much judicial activity in the summertime. This custom came about partially because South Carolina is an agricultural state and members of the jury just did not want to give up farming in order to go to court. Another reason for reduced activity in the summer was the fact that courthouses had no air conditioning and were hot and uncomfortable. In Spartanburg, Union and Gaffney, we held a little court in the month of May. Then, in the month of July, we held only enough criminal court to clear the jail. Defendants who were out on bond remained so until September, when a visiting judge rotated into the various circuits throughout the state.

When I came to practice law, and even for a few years after I served as circuit court judge, the courthouses remained open on Saturday morning until one o'clock. It was routine that circuit court judges went to the courthouse on Saturday morning for the purpose of hearing motions. These motions were heard in the town of the residence of the circuit judge and if, for example, lawyers from Gaffney and Union wanted to hear a motion on Saturday, they came to Spartanburg. Among the cases we would hear were domestic cases. Circuit court judges no longer take on these cases; they are heard exclusively by the family courts. In addition we would hear demurrers, motions for injunctions, or anything a judge could hear without the help of a jury. Until the early 1950s, lawyers maintained their offices on Saturday morning. After I came to practice law, a few lawyers opened their offices on Saturday afternoons. I am not aware of any lawyers who maintain Saturday office hours these days, but a few head into the office for the purpose of doing research with the doors locked.

Having completed my term of court in the summer of 1950 in my own home circuit, I rotated that fall into the third circuit, which was composed of Sumter, Williamsburg, Lee and Clarendon counties. From then on, over a period of 17 years, it was two circuits a year plus one at home in the summer. Under this system, it took seven years to travel the entire state. During this time, I would hold a series of courts in each of the 46 counties. In small counties such as Jasper and Lee, Edgefield and McCormick, there would be little court, but in large counties such as Charleston, Greenville, Spartanburg and Columbia, one never got caught up. I remember on one occasion driving to Charleston on 10 consecutive Sunday evenings and coming back to Spartanburg for the weekend. It was truly an exasperating assignment, but was compensated for by the fact that when I got to the small counties, often court would be called off or would adjourn by Tuesday at noon.

As I began traveling the state, I soon learned that the great masses of people have great respect for the court and for the judges who serve. When I would go to Greenville, Anderson, Florence, Columbia and Charleston, court made no big news. These counties held court nearly all the time. But when court opened in Hampton or Dillon, Walhalla or Pickens, Jasper or Beaufort, considerable news was made. It was an event to which many of the town's people, and certainly all the members of the bar, looked forward. The trial court on which I served was a court of general jurisdiction. We sometimes say it has unlimited jurisdiction. This means that we could try the important cases involving both civil and criminal matters including those that called for the death penalty.

Until 1973, the legislature was largely responsible for the court system. It not only elected the judges, but also determined by statutory law where and when terms of court would be conducted and what kind of court would be held. There were approximately 300 state statutes that were in effect rules of court. These were repealed in 1985. The system was truly asinine, because the setting of terms of court gave no consideration to the number of cases pending in the respective counties. I often stated when I was a circuit judge – and still believe – I was only half-employed because no one was charged with the duty of assigning me to the county where judicial work needed to be done. The court system was truly a hodgepodge.

In order to patch up the system, the various local legislative delegations would from time to time enact statutes creating courts below the circuit courts. These courts had such jurisdiction as the local legislators in their wisdom, or according to their whims, wanted the court to exercise. Most of the courts had jurisdiction over family problems. Jurisdiction was not exclusive, and one could bring family court problems in either a county or circuit court. It was conducive to judge shopping.

I had not been a circuit court judge long when I came to realize as never before that the administration of justice takes place at the trial court level. Appellate courts are necessary, but more than 99 percent of all litigation commences at the county courthouses and ends at the courthouses. I often have told my young friends that the place to practice law or make a living is in the office or in the county courthouse.

The circuit court system finally became so unsatisfactory that a movement began in the late 1960s and early 1970s to bring about a unified court system. The creation of this system is probably the most important thing that has taken place during my years at the bar.

Riding circuit was a truly interesting experience. Senator Strom Thurmond often said that a circuit court judge has the best office in the state, and I agree that there is no greater experience. In South Carolina, judges traditionally visited in the homes of lawyers and no one thought there was anything improper about it. I conclude, after talking to many judges from other states, that this was not the custom elsewhere.

I found that the habits that young lawyers develop are inspired by the older lawyers. Young lawyers observe what the older lawyers are doing. It was customary for all the members of the bar to do something for the visiting judge in a particular county; the young lawyers did the same. When a circuit judge moved into a circuit for a four-month stay, typically at the time of his departure, he would be entertained by the local bar with a banquet. It was always a nice party and sometimes the members of the bar roasted the judge, a friendly gesture that we always took in good humor.

We continue to use the rotation system under the new constitutional amendment, but the rotation is not as automatic as it used to be. Under the old system, I could tell four to seven years in advance where I would be on any given Monday. I would not know whether there would be any work for me on those particular Mondays, but I knew where our legislature had told me to be. The court administrator now studies the docket, based on reports that he receives from the various county clerks, and detects where the judge power is needed most urgently. This enables him to get a maximum of service out of each circuit court judge. Whereas there used to be a lot of half-employed judges, there are now none.

*Adapted from *Littlejohn's Half Century at the Bench and Bar (1936–1986).*

12 The Supreme Court's Personnel

Since 1930, there have been 16 chief justices of the Supreme Court of South Carolina. Chief Justice Richard Cannon Watts was elected chief justice in 1927 after the death of Chief Justice Pope. He served until 1931, the year of his death. Eugene Blease had served as an associate justice since 1926 and was elected chief justice in 1931, serving until his resignation in 1934. Traditionally, the senior associate justice was promoted to chief justice, but Blease ran out of turn and was elected. It has been reported that he was unpopular with the members of the court and was unhappy, resulting in his leaving the court and returning to Newberry to practice law in 1934. Since 1930, 27 lawyers have come to serve on the Supreme Court of South Carolina. The chief justices and associate justices with whom they worked are as follows:

(1) The Eugene Blease Court:
Thomas P. Cothran
John Stabler
Jesse Carter
Milledge Bonham

(2) The John G. Stabler Court:
Jesse Carter
Milledge Bonham
D. Gordon Baker
Ladson Fishburne

(3) The Milledge Bonham Court:
Jesse Carter
D. Gordon Baker
Ladson Fishburne
Taylor Stukes

(4) The D. Gordon Baker Court:
Ladson Fishburne
Taylor Stukes
Claude A. Taylor
Dewey Oxner

(5) The D. Gordon Baker court:
Taylor Stukes
Claude A. Taylor
Dewey Oxner
Lionel Legge

(6) The Taylor Stukes court:
Claude A. Taylor
Dewey Oxner
Lionel Legge
Joseph Moss

(7) The Claude A. Taylor Court:
Dewey Oxner
Lionel Legge
Joseph Moss
Woodrow Lewis

(8) The Claude A. Taylor Court:
James Brailsford
Joseph Moss
Woodrow Lewis
Thomas Bussey

(9) The Joseph Moss Court:
Woodrow Lewis
Thomas Bussey
James Brailsford
Bruce Littlejohn

(10) The Woodrow Lewis Court:
Thomas Bussey
Bruce Littlejohn
J.B. Ness
William Rhodes

(11) The Woodrow Lewis Court:
Bruce Littlejohn
J.B. Ness
William Rhodes
George Gregory

(12) The Woodrow Lewis Court:
Bruce Littlejohn
J.B. Ness
George Gregory
David Harwell

(13) The Bruce Littlejohn Court:
    J.B. Ness
    George Gregory
    David Harwell
    Lee Chandler

(14) The J.B. Ness Court
    George Gregory
    David Harwell
    Lee Chandler
    Ernest Finney

(15) The George Gregory Court:
    David Harwell
    Lee Chandler
    Ernest Finney
    Jean Toal

(16) The David Harwell Court:
    Lee Chandler
    Ernest Finney
    Jean Toal
    James Moore

(17) The A. Lee Chandler court:
    Ernest Finney
    Jeal Toal
    James Moore
    John Waller

(18) The Ernest Finney Court:
    Jean Toal
    James Moore
    John Waller
    E.C. Burnett III

(19) The Jean Toal Court:
    James Moore
    John Waller
    E.C. Burnett III
    Costa Pleicones

While 16 members of the Supreme Court of South Carolina served as chief justice, as indicated above, the court has changed some personnel a total of 18 times. Of the 27 justices who served on the court since 1930, 11 have not served as chief justice.

The new Supreme Court of South Carolina building, 1971

Inside the new supreme court hearing room, 1971

The Baker Court (Oxner, Stukes, Baker, Taylor, Legge) (L to R)

The Stukes Court (Legge, Taylor, Stukes, Oxner, Moss) (L to R)

The Taylor Court (Bussey, Moss, Taylor, Lewis, Brailsford) (L to R)

The Moss Court (Brailsford, Lewis, Moss, Bussey, Littlejohn) (L to R)

The Lewis Court (Rhodes, Littlejohn, Lewis, Ness, Gregory) (L to R)

The Littlejohn Court (Harwell, Ness, Littlejohn, Gregory, Chandler) (L to R)

The Ness Court (Chandler, Gregory, Ness, Harwell, Finney) (L to R)

The Gregory Court (Finney, Harwell, Gregory, Chandler, Toal) (L to R)

The Harwell Court (Toal, Chandler, Harwell, Finney, Moore) (L to R)

The Chandler Court (Moore, Finney, Chandler, Toal, Waller) (L to R)

The Finney Court (Waller, Toal, Finney, Moore, Burnett) (L to R)

The Toal Court (Burnett, Moore, Toal, Waller, Pleicones) (L to R)

First Court of the Appeals, 1983 (Goolsby, Bell, Gardner, Sanders, Shaw, Cureton) (L to R)

SECTION II

A JUDICIARY IN TRANSITION

13 The South Carolina Judicial Council

Prior to 1957, the S.C. Bar Association created several committees to study problems of the bench and bar and make recommendations to the S.C. Legislature and Supreme Court of South Carolina. The bar association had no official status. It was primarily a social organization, convening every summer and producing programs of general interest. Without official standing, its recommendations were not highly regarded and were often ignored.

Some at the bench and bar thought that an official organization should be set up to study problems within the administration of justice and make recommendations to the supreme court and/or legislature. Chief Justice Gordon Baker, who was inclined to resist change, vigorously opposed any such organization. Upon Baker's retirement, Associate Justice Taylor Stukes took over as chief. He was as vigorously in favor of the creation of the judicial council as Baker was opposed to it. By judicial directive, the new chief justice brought the S.C. Judicial Council into being. In 1977, it was given statutory recognition. Since then, it has served an important function.

The council is composed of the following:

(1) the chief justice of the Supreme Court of South Carolina or other designated member of the court;
(2) two circuit court judges of the state;
(3) two family court judges of the state;
(4) two probate judges of the state;
(5) the attorney general or one of the assistant attorneys general or one of the circuit solicitors;
(6) the dean or a member of the faculty of the University of South Carolina School of Law;
(7) the president of the S.C. Bar;
(8) the lieutenant governor (or designee);
(9) the speaker of the S.C. House of Representatives (or designee);
(10) the chairman of the S.C. Senate Finance Committee (or designee);
(11) the chairman of the S.C. House Ways and Means Committee (or designee);
(12) the chairman of the S.C. Senate Judiciary Committee (or designee);
(13) the chairman of the S.C. House Judiciary Committee (or designee);
(14) the director of the S.C. Legislative Council;
(15) six other members, of whom at least four must be members of the bar or this state;
(16) two judges of the magistrates' courts; and
(17) two masters-in-equity.

By reason of the several members who serve *ex officio*, and by reason of the high office that they occupy, the recommendations of the council have now come to be recognized and highly respected.

In 1958, the S.C. Judicial Council made a study of the rules of civil procedure and recommended the S.C. Legislature adopt a rules system similar to that approved in 1985. At that time, rule changes had to be approved by the general assembly. The council's recommendation was approved by the house but rejected in the senate by one vote. It was not until 27 years later that the rules were finally adopted. Known as the "South Carolina Rules of Civil Procedure," they became effective July 1, 1985. In similar fashion, the council has made a study of the appellate court rules, which have now also been adopted.

The rules of civil procedure and the appellate court now serve the bench and bar well. Prior to the adoption of these rules, both were controlled by statutory law, such rules of court as existed, and opinions of the supreme court. It was difficult for judges and lawyers to keep abreast of all they should know by researching these three sources for courtroom procedures.

14 Post-Conviction Relief Cases

In the 1960s, the Supreme Court of the United States held that the states must provide a forum wherein a person serving a sentence could contest incarceration. Such applications for relief are not a substitute for conventional appeals but, in effect, give a prisoner a chance to prove that he is being wrongfully held for some reason not reviewable in a conventional appeal. For some time, the courts in South Carolina were giving prisoners *habeas corpus* hearings or other types of applications for relief.

In 1962, the general assembly passed an act cited as the "Uniform Post-Conviction Procedure Act." This statute permits a prisoner to contest the constitutionality of state law, to contest jurisdiction to impose sentences, to claim that sentences exceed the maximum authorized by law, to claim that the sentence had expired, to claim that he was inadequately represented, and to claim several other alleged improper actions of the government to his detriment, all of which are more fully described in the statute itself.

The ruling of the Supreme Court of the United States and the statute itself increased the workload of all courts. It enabled the prisoner to have a hearing before the state trial judge, the state appellate court judges and the supreme court. After exhausting all the possibilities at the state level, the prisoner could start over and exhaust the possibilities at the federal level, including the Supreme Court of the United States a second time.

This ruling of the court and of statutory law delayed finalizing the validity of the sentence being served. The delay is especially apparent in death penalty cases. At the time of this writing, more than 3,500 death penalty cases were pending in the United States, with more than 70 death penalty cases pending in the state of South Carolina.

15 The Courts' Sentences

Perhaps the most solemn chore assigned to a trial judge is that of passing sentences in criminal cases. To a judge, it is daunting to know that the few words he will utter will determine the fate of the defendant – to wit, where he will spend his time. Until 1940, no probation and parole department existed in South Carolina government. Judges had much authority during sentencing, though they still had to operate within limits. A judge could sentence a defendant either to serve time on the county chain gang or in the state penitentiary. He also could direct him to pay a fine or he could pass a sentence and suspend it. Before 1941, the condition of the suspension was that he behave himself, but there was no entity assigned the duty of seeing that he did so. Then, during Governor Burnet Maybank's administration in 1941, the legislature created the probation and parole board. Today, there are some 30,000 persons on probation in South Carolina. The number far exceeds those who are actually serving time.

Prior to about 1972, most counties had a county chain gang. Spartanburg County had four. One of the principal chores of the chain gang was maintaining dirt roads. Prisoners would work along with large mules to pull a scrape over the surface, leveling out the irregularities.

Until recent times, prisons had no air conditioning. About 1972, Bill Leak, who headed the prison system, persuaded the legislature to abolish all chain gangs. He agreed to accept all of the prisoners and, I am told, lived to regret the decision. Today there are no chain gangs.

16 Changes – 1930 to 2004

Reference has been made throughout this history of the judiciary from 1930 to 2004 to the many changes that have taken place in the work of justices, judges and lawyers. In the early part of this history, there just wasn't much work for the 14 circuit court judges, five members of the supreme court and the 800 lawyers. There was plenty of work in 2004 for all of these, and many never get caught up. What is now known as workers' compensation came into being in 1935. This created a great deal of work for lawyers who practice in this area, thereby creating a great deal of work for all justices and judges.

In 1941, the legislature set up the probation and parole systems. It necessitated an increasingly large number of hearings relative to violations of probationary sentences. In the 1950s, the legislature passed laws requiring operators of motor vehicles to have liability insurance. Prior to that time, wreck cases often went unfiled because the culprit was unable to respond to a judgment. The new provision created much business for tort lawyers and, in turn, for the courts.

In *Gideon v. Wainwright* (a Florida case), the Supreme Court of the United States held that all defendants had a right to an attorney and that one must be appointed for indigent defendants. Gone are the days when a judge could simply accept the word of a defendant that he or she was guilty. Now a guilty plea requires some 20 to 30 minutes of interrogation by the judge to make sure the defendant understands his or her rights even though he or she has an attorney who would normally have explained the rights.

Plea bargaining has now been approved by the Supreme Court of the United States and, in turn, by state courts. In large measure, this shifts the sentencing authority to the office of the solicitor. Even though the judge does not have to accept the recommendation of the prosecuting officer relative to a plea, normally the judge does so in an effort to clear the dockets where many cases are ready for disposition.

New rules of court in both civil and criminal matters create additional work for lawyers and judges. In the past, summary judgments were not recognized in South Carolina. Today, judges must hear a multitude of such applications for relief. Discovery today is time-consuming and expensive. Post-conviction relief makes it necessary for the court administrator to set aside many weeks of court every year for the hearing of post-conviction relief applications. While few are granted relief, the hearings are time consuming. Divorces, which were prohibited by the South Carolina Constitution of 1895, came to be legal in 1949. Prior to that time, people had to leave the state to get a divorce or they just had to put up with each other. The amount of business created by the law of divorce presently requires the attention of 51 judges.

Appeals have become less expensive. Prior to about 1980, appellate records had to be printed. The printer charged $11 per page. The printers were gaining more than the litigants. Now appellate records need not be printed, making the cost of appeals less, which generates more appeals. Arbitration and mediation have come into being in recent years.

This does not minimize litigation, but it does eliminate the necessity of many trials. Capital cases are now more complicated, technical and involved. In days of yore, capital cases were treated as any other criminal case. The Supreme Court of the United States has, in effect, written the rules of procedure in all criminal cases and especially in capital cases.

These are just a few of the many developments at law that have caused South Carolina to establish family courts, to add 32 more circuit courts and to create the court of appeals. It is inescapable in this age of activity, where people go places and do things, that more lawsuits will be filed. In like fashion, it is inescapable that more crime is being committed, necessitating the services of judges at all levels.

17 Everything Changes

Recently, I pointed out to one of my young lawyer friends one of the changes that has been brought about in the legal and judicial world since I began practicing law in 1936. My friend said, "Judge, there is no use in pointing out any one thing that is different; actually, everything is different." I am inclined to agree with my young friend. To begin with, the process of becoming a lawyer in 1936 was far simpler. To get into law school, all I had to do was write a letter to the dean telling him that I had completed three years at Wofford College and wanted to go to law school. He replied promptly to my application and told me to bring a copy of my transcript and show up on September 2, 1933.

At that time, one did not need to be a graduate of an undergraduate college. Three years was sufficient; occasionally they would even let a student in after two years. The dean also told me that the tuition for law school would be $50 per semester and that I could rent a room on campus for $20 per semester. Contrast this with the cost of going to law school today, which runs into many thousands of dollars every semester. After I had finished law school and received my diploma, it was not necessary to stand a state bar examination. I received my diploma from law school on June 2, was sworn in by Chief Justice Stabler along with 17 other students on June 3 and on June 10, I opened my office and was ready to practice any kind of law needed by clients I might be able to entice to come to my office.

I was ready to practice law – after all, why shouldn't I? I had a diploma. I had a certificate. I had gone by Young Office Supply and bought a yellow pad and a pencil with an eraser. That is all one needed to practice law in 1936. We had no ballpoint pens, no electric type-writers, no word processors, no copying machines, no fax machines, no air conditioning, no dial telephone. My telephone number was 64. If one attempted to practice law with only a yellow pad and a pencil to-day, he would be somewhat like a call girl without a telephone trying to do business. All of the devices I enumerated above are today absolutely necessary to the practice of law.

At a recent meeting of the S.C. Bar in Charleston, there came into being what we know as the "Nifty Fifty Club." All lawyers who have been at the bar more than 50 years are eligible to join. I discovered to my amazement that I have outlived all the members of the bar except two. Only Henry Hammer and J.D. Todd were members when I came to Spartanburg and opened my office in 1936.[1]

Not only have the trappings of practicing law changed, the fo-cus has likewise. The day of specialization has come. Today, one really needs to be a specialist to practice law in the state and federal courts. The Supreme Court of South Carolina has recognized this by establish-ing a specialization program, such that one who wants to be a specialist can qualify by meeting certain requirements. The modern-day gradu-ate of law school is barely prepared to begin the practice of law.

The law clerk program is excellent because it enables about 50 law clerks and/or staff attorneys each year to complete their education by working with an active judge for one or two years. In actuality, I have been in favor of an internship for young lawyers. The doctors are ahead of us in this regard. Through a residency program, young doctors com-plete their education by working with older doctors for at least a year. Well, I began by saying that everything is different and I conclude by repeating that statement. Everything is different. Hopefully it is better – though I'm not at all sure of this.

[1] Henry Hammer passed away in August 2005 at age 94.

18 Workers' Compensation

Prior to 1935, a good portion of a circuit judge's work involved try-ing cases wherein an employee hurt on the job sued his employer. Such lawsuits created a difficult situation because once an employee sued the

employer, he often lost his job. Forty-six of 48 states had already enacted workmen's compensation laws. South Carolina and Mississippi
had not. Employers were generally in favor of a workmen's compensation law in South Carolina and lobbied diligently for a statute creating
a workmen's commission.

The enactment of this law relieved circuit courts of a great deal of
civil litigation. Governor Olin D. Johnston was not strongly in favor
of the law but signed it in July of 1935, appointing five commission-
ers to hear cases of employees injured on the job. A great many lawyers
who had represented employees in their claims against employers were
opposed to the statute. They rationalized that it would negatively affect
their business volume. Little did they realize at the time that practice of
law in front of the industrial commission would be much more lucra-
tive than attempting to win jury verdicts.

The value of money at that time is reflected in the fact that the act
provided as follows: "The total compensation payable under this Article shall in no case exceed $6,000.00." An award for disfigurement was
limited to $2,500. The five commissioners were each paid $3,000 per
year and received five cents per mile when they traveled away from the
home base in Columbia. Over the years, the benefits have increased
proportionate to inflation. Today, the salary of a workers' compensation commissioner is almost equivalent to that of a circuit court judge.
While the office of a circuit judge is considered more prestigious than
that of a workers' compensation commissioner, it is likely that each industrial commissioner today controls more discretionary money than
any one circuit court judge and his jury.

19 Demonstrative Evidence at the Washington Street Theatre

For many years prior to World War II, there was practically no demonstrative evidence introduced in the trial of cases. Occasionally, one
might have a picture of a wreck scene or something of that sort. Perhaps the inspiration for presenting demonstrative evidence to a jury
came from the fact that the army during World War II emphasized the
desirability of teaching by way of demonstration. It was the army's the-
ory that one retains 80 percent of what one sees and only 12 percent
of what one hears. Lawyers coming back from the army came to realize

that they needed to persuade jurors of much in a short period of time. Seeing became as important as hearing.

A newsworthy example of demonstrative evidence occurred in the Supreme Court of South Carolina in 1972. A theatre operator from Darlington was convicted of showing pornographic movies in violation of the statute. On appeal, it was the request of counsel for both the state and the defendant that the full court see the entire movie. Miss Frances Smith, the court's clerk, rented the Washington Street Theatre one afternoon for the viewing by the court. The film left nothing to the imagination. The conviction of the defendant was affirmed.

This may be the only time during this period of history that a movie was shown in a theater to members of the supreme court. It was the last word in demonstrative evidence.

20 Bastions of the Status Quo

Over the years, many courtroom traditions endured because that was the way it was done in England two or three centuries ago. Most people say they are in favor of reform but in actuality don't want to be bothered with change. The older lawyers are content to do things as they always have, assuming an attitude to the effect that, "I don't want to be bothered with anything different." The young lawyers have too little influence to bring about change. I think, for example, of the old practice of placing a prisoner in the dock in order to arraign him. After the defendant pleaded not guilty, the clerk asked him, "How will you be tried?" (As if his answer would make any difference.) Miraculously, all of the defendants chose the same way for trial. Upon advice of counsel, they would say, "by God and my country."

Many of the forms for indictments in this state must have been brought over on the *Mayflower* and no one bothered to change them. The indictment form used for more than 100 years was typically as follows:

"The Grand Jury Presents: That John Doe on the 27th day of October in the year of our Lord one thousand nine hundred and fifty-seven with force and arms, at Richland County Court House in the County of Richland and State of South Carolina, in and upon one Richard Roe feloniously, willfully and of his malice aforethought, did make an assault, and that the said John Doe him the said Richard Roe then and there feloniously, willfully and of his malice aforethought with one Pistol did shoot and wound; giving to the said Richard Roe thereby and upon the body of him the said Richard Roe one mortal wound; of which said mortal wound the said Richard Roe died. And so the Jurors aforesaid, upon their oath aforesaid, do say that the said John Doe him the said Richard Roe then and there, in the manner and by the means aforesaid, feloniously, willfully and of his malice aforethought, did kill and murder against the form of the Statute, in such case made and provided, and against the peace and dignity of the State."

One hundred years ago it was customary to allege that the crime occurred "with force and arms at the court house" and until the 1970s our indictments read the same way. I was amused to learn that a jury found a defendant "not guilty" because the solicitor had not proven that the incident took place at the courthouse as the indictment alleged. Other indictments were similarly cumbersome, and it was sometimes difficult to determine in a rape case who was the rapist and who the raped.

In the early 1970s, the judges, at their annual judicial conference, appointed Circuit Court Judge Lewis Rosen and Associate Attorney General J.C. Coleman to recommend changes in the many indictments used in this state and report back to the conference the following August. They did an excellent job and proposed the rewriting of all the indictments. They came up with the following, which is entirely sufficient and has never been challenged: "It is alleged that the Defendant, John Doe, did in Richland County on or about October 27, 1957, feloniously, willfully, and with malice aforethought, kill one Richard Roe, by poisoning, and that the victim died as a proximate result thereof, all in violation of §16-3-0010, 0020, *The South Carolina Code of Laws* (1976, as amended). Against the peace and dignity of the State, and contrary to the statute in such case made and provided." Judges had known for a long time that the indictments should be reformed. Fortunately, the South Carolina Judicial Conference decided to do something about it.

21 Judge Elected – By a Landslide

Since the Constitution of 1895, and perhaps before, members of the supreme court and of the circuit courts have been elected at a joint meeting of the S.C. House of Representatives and the S.C. Senate. Traditionally, judges who were unopposed were reelected early in the legislative session of the year in which their term expired. While judges of the state courts were never elected for life (as were federal court judges), once judges were elected, seldom have they been opposed. There are a few exceptions.

At the joint meeting, the presiding officer is the president of the senate who, traditionally, is also the lieutenant governor of the state. The speaker of the house sits alongside him but has no part in the proceeding. Something unusual occurred at a joint meeting of the house and senate called for the purpose of electing judges on January 12, 1949. Several judges were elected or reelected by unanimous consent. Duncan Bellinger, circuit judge of the fifth circuit, was up for reelection. No opposition had been announced. It was expected that his reelection would be routine. Judge Bellinger had a reputation for passing substantial sentences in criminal court. It was also said that no judge would give you a more fair trial than Bellinger. Lawyers dreaded his sentences. Among those delegates serving in the house from Greenville County was John Bolt Culbertson. He was an attorney who represented many defendants in criminal court and had experienced the long sentences usually imposed by the Fifth Circuit Court. Judge Bellinger was nominated by the senator from Richland County. Then someone moved that the nominations be closed and that the judge be elected by acclamation. Culbertson addressed the presiding officer and said, "I object."

I was aware of the fact that the constitution required that the roll be called unless an election was unanimous. The lieutenant governor turned to me and asked, "What do we do now?" "We have to call the roll," I replied. The roll was called and Culbertson voted for John Doe. Matthew Poliakoff of Spartanburg voted for Rhea Haskell. Thirty-seven members of the senate voted for Bellinger. One hundred twenty-one house members voted for Bellinger. The presiding officer announced that Bellinger had been elected by a vote of 158 to two.

Senator McLeod addressed the lieutenant governor and asked that the vote be deleted. The presiding officer ruled that the motion was out of order and that any member of the house or senate could vote for anyone they wanted. On at least two other occasions, judges who expected to be unopposed were the victims of substantial votes but none were defeated. Representative Haskell had a good sense of humor. After the joint session adjourned, he commented, "I concede the election."

22 Resignations

In 1952, the state constitution provided that the salary of a justice or judge may not be reduced or increased during the term for which he or she was elected. Associate Justice Taylor Stukes, Circuit Court Judges T.B. Greneker and Henry Johnson were reelected January 9, 1952, without opposition. The time had come when members of the house and senate recognized that the judges were not being adequately paid. Governor James F. Byrnes was in accord. Leadership of the general assembly, together with Governor Byrnes and Chief Justice D. Gordon Baker, devised a plan to get around the constitution. I participated in the plan but have never been too proud of the fact that I did. I was a new kid on the block, having only been in office two years, and was greatly influenced by the chief justice.

The leadership of the senate and house agreed that if justices and judges would resign they would be reelected without opposition. This would permit all to enter upon a new term and the salary could be increased without violating the letter of the constitution. The journals of the house and senate recite a letter from Governor Byrnes dated February 20, 1952, addressed to the presiding officers of the house and senate notifying them that Chief Justice D. Gordon Baker, Associate Justices Ladson Fishburne, Claude Taylor and Dewey Oxner of the Supreme Court of South Carolina had resigned. The letter further stated that Circuit Court Judges James M. Brailsford, Henry Henderson, Frank Eatmon, Joseph Moss, Bruce Littlejohn and Robert Martin had resigned. On that same day all of those who had resigned were reelected by acclamation. Circuit Court Judge Steve Griffith of the eighth circuit, in a letter addressed to the house and senate, indicated that he was not in accord.

The constitution has now been amended such that judicial salaries may not be reduced during the term for which judges are elected, but may be increased. The salary of the justices and judges deemed to be inadequate was $10,000 per year. It is my recollection that the governor was being paid $12,000 per year. As the justices entered upon a new term, they were paid $12,750 per year. Corresponding salaries (when this was written) are approximately $100,000 annually.

23 A Miserable Marathon

A history of the South Carolina judiciary from 1930 to 2004 would not be complete without a recitation of the unusual contest for a seat on the Supreme Court of South Carolina in 1966 and 1967. I was first elected a circuit judge in 1949 and had ridden circuit for a total of 17 years. It had never occurred to me that I might run for the Supreme Court because Chief Justice Claude A. Taylor and I both lived in the City of Spartanburg. It was not likely that the assembly would elect two of the five members of the supreme court from the same town. Judge J.B. Ness of the second circuit had been riding circuit since 1958. He had dreamed of going on the Supreme Court of South Carolina and had well-advertised his candidacy for some time. During that era, one could solicit votes and get commitments in advance from members of the assembly and there was no screening process.

In January 1966, Chief Justice Taylor had a massive heart attack and died. He was only 64 years of age – eight years short of retirement. His death caused me to rethink the matter, and I promptly announced that I would be a candidate to fill the vacancy. Judge Ness announced his candidacy also, as did Senator Rembert Dennis of Moncks Corner and former Governor George Bell Timmerman Jr. of Lexington. About a month after the death of Chief Justice Taylor, the house and senate passed a resolution providing for an election to fill the vacancy. For some reason I do not recall, the resolution provided that the assembly would convene every Wednesday at noon and cast three ballots until some candidate received a majority of the votes.

At the first meeting for the election, I received a total of 66 votes; Judge Ness received 57, Senator Dennis 32 and George Bell Timmerman Jr. eight. On the second roll call, the vote froze as did the vote on the third roll call. Throughout the session and until the assembly adjourned in May, it met every Wednesday and either called the roll three times or unanimously agreed to forego the second and third votes. A total of 36 ballots were cast before the general assembly adjourned in May. This meant that the election would have to be held the following January in 1967 when a new assembly took office.

That was a year for both the house members and the senators to be running for reelection. There was an unusual turnover of the membership. Come January 1967, there were 64 new faces in the legislature.

For the first time a substantial number of Republicans gained office in the summer of 1966 – a total of 23. Senator Dennis withdrew from the race as did former Governor Timmerman, who decided to seek a circuit court judgeship. During that summer, 315 persons sought the 170 seats in the assembly. I felt compelled to write each a letter. I did not want the day to come when some new member would say, "Bruce, I didn't know you were running."

The withdrawal of Dennis and Timmerman meant that there had to be an election on the next ballot unless there were a tie. When the roll was called, I received 105 votes and Judge Ness received 64. The next day after the election, Judge Ness made an announcement: "I am running for the supreme court for the next vacancy that occurs." He had to ride circuit for the next seven years until the retirement of Justice Brailsford. By that time, Judge Ness had enough commitments to assure his election, and he was named to the supreme court without opposition.

Friends are amazed that the miserable marathon which Judge Ness and I experienced did not affect our friendship. In good humor, we rationalized from time to time: "The trouble between us is we both want to marry the same woman, and she can't have but one of us." Justice Ness died in November 1991. He left instructions with the mortician that I be asked to take part in his funeral service, and I was privileged to do so.

24 Judges' and Lawyers' Education

By the early 1970s, many of us at the bench and bar had come to realize that ours was an antiquated system. The judges were more conscious of this than any other group, and they wanted to do something about it. Throughout the country there had developed an intense interest in improving the skills and competency of the bench and bar. More outspoken on the subject than any other was Chief Justice Warren Burger of the Supreme Court of the United States. On several occasions, he advertised the fact that he was unhappy with the education that law schools were giving to students all over the United States.

In 1968, speaking to the Phi Alpha Delta Legal Fraternity, Chief Justice Burger said, "The modern law school is failing in its basic duties to provide society with people-oriented and problem-oriented counselors and advocates to meet these broad social needs." Continuing the scathing denunciation, he stated, "The shortcoming of today's law graduate lies not in a deficient knowledge of law but that he has little, if any training in dealing with *facts* – the stuff of which *cases* are made. It is a rare law graduate, for example, who knows how to ask questions – simple, single questions, one at a time in order to develop facts in evidence. And a lawyer who cannot do that cannot do his tasks properly."

Chief Justice Burger's leadership caused a clamor that resulted in efforts to improve not only lawyer competency but the judicial system altogether. The judges of South Carolina joined the effort to improve the administration of justice by supporting a proposed amendment to the S.C. Constitution creating the unified judicial court system. This amendment, approved in 1972 and ratified in 1973, gave to the Supreme Court of South Carolina the authority to determine who practices law in the state. The court, by way of its rules, sets forth the qualifications of one admitted to practice law. Its rules require that members of the bar must stand and pass an examination offered twice yearly under the direction of six bar examiners. Applicants must be graduates of a law school accredited by the American Bar Association.

Until the early 1950s, a lawyer who read law in the office of a member of the bar for a period of two years could be certified by that lawyer to stand the bar. This system of gaining admission to the bar was rejected by the legislature in 1952. Several years later, the supreme court abolished the rule of comity. Under this rule, a lawyer who had practiced law for a number of years in another state could be admitted to practice in South Carolina without an examination. The court now requires such an applicant to take the bar examination and be approved by the Character and Fitness Committee, which has the duty of reviewing all applicants for admission.

About 1985, the court began requiring that all applicants for admission attend a Bridge the Gap Program. This program was administered by J.B. Ness, chief justice of the Supreme Court of South Carolina, until his death in 1991. In its programs, Chief Justice Ness was able to call upon the best judges and the best lawyers in the state to advise the students how to act and what to do when clients start walking through the door. Those who lectured at these programs gave to the students the benefit of their experiences, a benefit usually not available from law school professors.

The court required all judges coming under the unified court system to attend continuing judicial education programs periodically. These programs have done much to keep the judges abreast of current issues in the administration of justice. In days of yore, one newly admitted to the bar could go into court the next day and try a case, without ever having seen a case tried. One lawyer told me that he tried the first case he had ever seen tried. The court now requires that, prior to the appearance by a new lawyer alone in court, he or she must have observed trials in the court of general sessions, the court of common pleas, the family court and an equity court.

The supreme court now provides an orientation program for all newly elected judges and provides the new judges of the circuit courts a charge book. The chief justice now assigns newly elected judges to sit with a senior judge for two weeks before taking regular assignments in his or her own right.

The supreme court has enacted a code of ethics that sets forth the standards expected for members of the judiciary. Even as the court has the authority to admit persons to practice law, it can also disbar, suspend or otherwise sanction lawyers who misbehave. The authority to admit persons to practice law is virtually unlimited. It could, for example, permit high school graduates to be members of the profession. The court, however, has been meticulous in its efforts to see that only truly qualified persons come to practice law in our state.

A great portion of the judges coming under the unified court system have been sent to the National Judicial College in Reno, Nevada. This institution takes newly elected judges from throughout the country for a two-week, three-week or four-week program, orienting them and educating them to the techniques of operating an efficient court.

In August of every year, the supreme court calls into session the South Carolina Judicial Conference. The appellate court judges and the judges of the trial courts are members of the conference. Usually in attendance are the clerks and staff attorneys serving the many courts. The programs are well planned and assist all present in keeping up with what is new and different at the law.

25 The South Carolina Judicial Conference

Prior to the new Article V Judicial Section of the S.C. Constitution, ratified in 1973, all judges were *prima donnas* in their own right, answerable only to their conscience and their God. There was no administrative head of the judicial system. Such inherent and/or statutory power as the chief justice possessed was seldom, if ever, exercised. The legislature elected the circuit judges and determined by statute where court would be held in the various counties. Over the years, special courts and county courts were created in the larger counties, bringing about a hodgepodge court system.

In 1968, the supreme court came to realize that there was no structural opportunity for judges to meet to discuss problems of mutual interest. To remedy this, the court created the S.C. Judicial Conference and called its first meeting the latter part of August 1968. At that time, there were only 14 circuit court judges and five members of the supreme court. In attendance at the first conference were only 19 judges plus Miss Frances Smith, the clerk of the supreme court. The exchange of views proved fruitful and the conference has met every August now for more than 30 years. Like most governmental institutions, the conference has grown. Today, we find five members of the supreme court, nine members of the court of appeals, 46 circuit court judges, 51 family court judges, plus law clerks and staff attorneys, for a total of approximately 250 persons assigned duties incidental to the administration of justice.

These meetings are well planned and highly organized. While the purpose of the conference is to study problems of mutual interest, traditionally there are two nights of social functions, one of which is usually sponsored by the Richland County Bar Association. The convention provides a forum for the exchange of ideas, and alerts those present of changes in substantive and procedural law. Every year, there are many topics needing discussion.

The creation of the conference was loudly applauded by members of the bar. Attorney Douglas McKay Jr., writing in the bar's publication, said, "The Conference will meet at least once every calendar year. Its next formal meeting is scheduled for two days commencing the 28th of August, 1969 in the Supreme Court Room. One of the items on the agenda is the revision and amendment of the Rules of the Circuit Court, and the formulation of new Rules." The creation of the judicial conference should be applauded by the members of the bar, and by the public it serves. It provides a forum for evaluation of new concepts in procedure and revisiting old concepts in need of updating. The supreme court has now adopted new rules affecting practice in both the appellate courts and in the circuit courts. These are of great interest to attorneys who try cases in the circuit courts and argue appeals in the appellate courts.

The S.C. Judicial Conference now plays an important part in keeping those who work within the unified court system abreast of what is new.

26 Unified Court System

Many of us at the bench and bar, and laypeople too, recognized during the 1950s and 1960s that the administration of justice in South Carolina was not what it ought to be. There was much talk of reform, but no significant changes were brought about until the constitution was amended in 1973. The chief justice of the supreme court had, by reason of statute, authority to bring about many improvements in the court system, but nothing was done about it until 1973 because the legislature never provided administrative money to bring about reform. After many debates, studies and committee meetings of the bench and bar, significant amendments to the judicial department section of the S.C. Constitution were proposed. The people approved the amendments in the fall of 1972. They were ratified by the general assembly in the spring of 1973. Prior to 1973, the judicial system of South Carolina worked like rudderless ship. Circuit court judges were answerable to no one.

The most significant amendment was simple and short. It provided: "The judicial power shall be vested in a unified judicial system, which shall include a Supreme Court, a Circuit Court, and such other courts of uniform jurisdiction as may be provided for by general law."

Other portions of the judicial amendment directed the chief justice to appoint an administrator of the court and such assistants as were deemed necessary to aid in the administration of the courts of the state. The chief justice was empowered to set the terms of circuit court and to appoint any judge within the unified court system to serve on any court of the system. It further gave to the supreme court administrative rule-making authority and also gave the court jurisdiction over admission to the practice of law and the discipline of attorneys. William Dallas served as the first court administrator. He was appointed by Chief Justice Joseph R. Moss.

More recently, the judicial department section of our constitution has been amended to require that applicants for judge be screened. The screening authority may approve three candidates as being eligible for each judicial office up for election.

A unified system is difficult, if not impossible, to define. Generally it can be said that various court activities must be uniform. Perhaps it would be accurate to say that the unified court system is that which the supreme court deems it to be. After the constitution was amended in 1973, the legislature continued to enact statutes creating judges and/or courts, but statewide uniformity was lacking. Attorney General McLeod brought an action in the original jurisdiction of the supreme court to contest the authority of the legislature to enact laws which were not uniform. In a single opinion, the court held that the 32 courts with jurisdiction more than a magistrate but less than a circuit judge were unconstitutional and were abolished. Cases pending in those courts were transferred to the circuit court.

The ruling of the court took the bar and a multitude of people by surprise. When the constitutional amendment was proposed and ratified, no one envisioned its true impact. The ruling of this court was necessary in order to bring the court system into constitutional unity, but the lobby to oppose the amendment might have been overbearing. Understandably, the workload of the circuit courts was greatly increased such that additional circuit judges were needed.

The unified court amendment brought about many changes in the administration of justice in South Carolina. The system now seems to be working well in spite of the fact that the caseload in all courts has increased and apparently will continue to increase.

27 Assault on Judicial Reform

For many years prior to 1972, members of the bench and bar had been dreaming of the day when the judicial section of the state constitution would be repealed and a more modern version adopted. The advocates of reform completed the work on the new article V of the constitution in the spring of 1972. The proposal received the required 82 votes in the house and 32 votes in the senate. Constitutional amendments are usually adopted by the voters without great debate.

After the assembly adjourned, the solicitors, coroners, clerks of court and sheriffs realized much to their dismay that the proposed amendment did not provide for them to be elected by the people in a general election. They decided to oppose the proposed amendment. Whether the provision had been left out of the proposed amendment by accident or by design is hard to say. Those who advocated the addition of the amendment recognized that 16 solicitors, 46 sheriffs, 46 coroners and 46 clerks of court could have substantial influence with the voters and could conceivably cause the amendment's defeat.

Most people hesitate to give up the right to elect public officials. This is true even though often they don't understand the duties and responsibilities of the officeholders involved. The argument that the people would now be deprived of the right to elect these four officeholders held much appeal. Advocates of the amendment were greatly concerned. Members of the bench and bar as well as members of the legislature did not want to risk the possibility of having the people vote against the amendment. They made a deal with the solicitors, the coroners, the clerks of court and the sheriffs that if they would support the amendment, a further amendment restoring these four offices to the electorate would be proposed, submitted and supported in the general election of 1974. In 1974 the amendment was proposed, approved by the general assembly and approved by the people in the November election. It was ratified in the spring of 1975. Rejection of the 1972 amendment was averted and all parties concerned came away happy with the final result.

28 Women: Judges, Lawyers and Jurors

During the period in judicial history that this book covers, women have come to play an important part in the administration of justice. The 1942 *Code of Laws for South Carolina* included a short provision enacted in 1918, providing that women be allowed to practice law in South Carolina under the same terms and conditions as men. Prior thereto, it can be assumed that it was debatable as to whether women could become attorneys. It must have been that the supreme court had refused to admit women and the legislature determined to do something about it.

The first woman to practice law in South Carolina was James "Miss Jim" M. Perry from Greenville. She was admitted in 1918. By 1932, there was a sprinkling of female students at the University of South Carolina School of Law. During the years I was at the law school (1933–1936), only three women were in attendance. One graduated. It was not until about 1960 that women in large numbers began applying for admission to the various law schools throughout the country.

I read recently in the *American Bar Association Journal* that, of the approximately 125,000 students in the accredited law schools in the United States, about 47,000 are women. This represents 38 percent of the students in the 175 accredited law schools. It is my understanding that many law schools today have more female students than males. In South Carolina it is estimated that 30 percent of the practicing attorneys are women. They are now serving in judicial offices as well.

The part that women play in the administration of justice in South Carolina is demonstrated by several elections. In 1988, Jean H. Toal became the first woman elected to the supreme court. In 2000, she was made chief justice. In 2004, she received the Margaret Brent Women Lawyers of Achievement Award, the highest honor bestowed by the American Bar Association of Women Lawyers, during the ABA Annual Convention in Atlanta, Georgia. In 1999, Kaye G. Hearn, who previously served as a family court judge, was elected chief judge of the S.C. Court of Appeals. She served with Carol Connor, a member of the court of appeals, for several years prior to Judge Connor's death in 2004. In 1993, Elaine Fowler was elected the first woman president of the S.C. Bar.

Some interesting statistics are recited in the spring 2002 issue of *The Briefcase*, the newsletter of the S.C. Women Lawyers Association. It stated that women comprise 27 percent of the bar's members – 2,831 of the 10,568 bar members. The article goes on to indicate that women are also making progress in the judicial arena. Female judges at each judicial level requiring a law degree are as follows: supreme court, 1; court of appeals, 2; circuit court, 4; family court, 14; and administrative law judge, 1 – a total of 22 women serving in a judicial capacity above the level of magistrate. The article goes further to indicate that

45 percent of the applicants to the University of South Carolina School of Law are women and 43 percent of those enrolled are also women. Clearly women are making consistent inroads to the legal profession in South Carolina

Ruth Williams Cupp, a prominent Charleston attorney, has published a book that includes biographical sketches of the first 100 women coming to practice law in South Carolina. She indicates that Barbara Burt Brown of Spartanburg was the 33rd woman admitted to the bar – in December 1940. The 100th woman lawyer to be admitted to the bar occurred in 1972. The book is entitled *Portia Steps Up to the Bar.* Truly, women have become an important cog in the wheel of the administration of Justice in South Carolina.

Prior to the spring of 1967, women were not allowed to serve on juries in South Carolina. The statutory law of the state said that juries would be composed of men only. The United States Supreme Court held that the jury box must contain the names of a cross section of the population including women. The statutory law of the state was amended and today it is not unusual for a majority of the members of a jury to be composed of women. They are serving the court system in South Carolina well.

SECTION III

THE MODERN COURT

29 Family Courts and Divorces

The Constitution of 1895 prohibited divorces in South Carolina. From 1895 until 1949, unhappy couples had to endure or, in some instances, establish an actual or fictitious residence in another state and procure a foreign divorce. From 1895 to 1948, attorneys and other members of the general assembly would propose an amendment to the constitution permitting divorces. They were unable to round up the 82 votes in the house and 32 votes in the senate necessary to submit the question of divorce to the people in a general election. After World War II, members of the general assembly took a different view. In November 1948, at the general election, the people approved the proposed amendment. The assembly ratified the amendment in the spring of 1949.

The fact that divorces were not permitted for a little over half a century did not mean that there were no domestic problems to be handled by the court. During that time, actions could still be brought for separate maintenance and child custody and support. Circuit judges had jurisdiction to try these cases but a great portion of them were heard in local courts of lesser jurisdiction. In addition, by statute, it was a criminal offense for an able-bodied husband and/or father to desert and/or fail to support his wife and minor children. Under this statute, a wife, mother or other person could procure a criminal warrant and the grand jury would treat the matter like any other criminal case. The case would be tried before a judge and jury. Usually it would result in a guilty plea and a probationary sentence with a condition of the probation being that the defendant pay a certain amount of money either directly to the wife or to the clerk of court. The statute provided a poor vehicle for the collection of money.

From 1949 until 1977, cases were more often referred to the master-in-equity or to a referee. Over the years, circuit court judges and inferior courts were increasingly burdened with this litigation. After the ratification in 1973 of the new reform amendment to the constitution, which provided for a unified court system, the legislature made a study of the needs of the state in the family court area. This resulted in the creation of the family court system by a statute enacted in 1976. The family courts came to have sole jurisdiction over cases involving divorce, child custody, separate maintenance, alimony, adoption, change of name and criminal cases where juveniles were charged with crimes. Under this arrangement, 46 family court judges were elected. All cases are tried in equity by a family court judge without a jury. The establishment of these courts is one of the most significant changes brought about in my experience at the bench and bar. Without the family courts, circuit courts would be hopelessly inundated with litigation. As of this writing, the number of family court judges has increased to 51. It is their task to keep peace in the family or dissolve the family peacefully.

In the early 1980s, the supreme court adopted a rule, already in effect in most other states, permitting a family court judge to divide marital property equitably. This is now an important part of the court's work. The new rule gives the judge authority to substitute for a jury and divide property accumulated during the time of the marriage. It can be forcefully argued that every family court judge controls more discretionary money and property than any circuit court judge and jury combined.

It seems to be in the scheme of things that more actions are brought in the family courts every year. According to the National Center for Health Statistics and the U.S. Census Bureau, upwards of half of marriages end in divorce. There is little reason to believe that fewer family court judges will be needed in the future. More likely there will be a need for more.

Family court judges are elected at a joint session of the house and senate, as are circuit court judges and members of appellate courts. All are subject to the same screening process. These judges are assigned to a judicial circuit but rotate around the entire state at the discretion of the chief justice. Increasingly, problems are assigned to family court to solve. There are no half-employed family court judges.

30 The Chief Justice Lewis Administration

Circuit court judge, associate justice and later Chief Justice J. Woodrow Lewis of Darlington brought to the office a broad background of legal experiences. For some 15 years, he rode circuit; for about 15 years, he served as associate justice and then became chief justice in the summer of 1975. This was two years after the people had amended Article V of the state constitution mandating a unified court system. Chief Justice Lewis succeeded Chief Justice Joseph R. Moss. Chief Justice Moss had been a circuit court judge, an associate justice and served as chief justice for approximately nine years. He well understood and was anxious to see an improvement of the South Carolina court system. He followed the recommendations of the S.C. Bar but was not one to initiate changes himself. On the other hand, Chief Justice Lewis saw a need for change and was ready, willing and able to do something about it. He provided leadership for the bench and bar, and was content to lock horns with the general assembly as related to the powers and authority of the judicial department contrasted with the powers and authority of the general assembly.

The Judicial Reform Constitutional Amendment approved by the people in the fall of 1972 and ratified by the legislature in 1973 mandated a unified court system but did not spell out just what power and authority the amendment authorized. Perhaps it may be said that a unified court system has such powers as the court determines.

The crying need for court rule changes had been there for many years. Bar and court committees had been studying rule changes since as far back as 1958. Prior to adoption of the new Article V, it had been generally considered that the legislature could enact court rules. Article V, paragraph 4 provided in relevant part as follows: "The Supreme Court shall make rules governing the administration of all the courts of the State. Subject to the statutory law, the Supreme Court shall make rules governing the practice and procedure in all such courts."

For many years one needed to look three places to find out how to try a case. The more than 300 statutes were, in effect, court rules. The supreme court issued some 100 of those. There also were a multitude of supreme court decisions indicating courtroom procedures. Lawyers and judges craved a reference wherein all of the rules of court could be found. Considerable negotiations took place between Chief Justice Lewis and Senator Marion Gressette. The senator had been in office for approximately 45 years, was chair of the senate judiciary committee and was very protective of his assumed rights to influence court activities. While there was little hope that the authority to make rules could be resolved, it was well understood that the general assembly was a very poor organization to enact court rules.

On August 31, 1982, the supreme court issued a scholarly order prepared by Chief Justice Lewis and signed by all members of the supreme court. The order spelled out in no uncertain terms that the authority to make rules was held by the Supreme Court of South Carolina. This infuriated many members of the general assembly, especially Senator Gressette. At an ensuing meeting of the general assembly, the legislature proposed a constitutional amendment denying the supreme court rule-making authority and vesting the authority in the general assembly. The proposed amendment was approved by more than 82 members of the house and more than 32 members of the senate. It appeared that the proposed constitutional amendment would be voted upon by the people in November 1984 and approved.

In more sober moments, the Speaker of the House Robert Sheheen advocated voiding the proposed amendment and substituting a proposed amendment that would give the supreme court the authority to initiate rules, and the general assembly the authority to veto the rules by a three-fifths majority vote of the two houses. The supreme court agreed to this. The people approved the Sheheen proposal and it was ratified in the spring of 1985. The amendment has worked well. The supreme court now initiates all rule changes, many of which have been sent to the assembly, but none vetoed.

It is to the credit of the administration of Chief Justice Lewis that he took a system that was like a rudderless ship and put organization into it. Except for the unified court system, which has now been in place for more than 20 years, the administration of justice would be in chaos. On March 8, 1985, Chief Justice Lewis turned 72 and was required by the rules of the court to retire. During that same week Senator Gressette died. The relationship between the judicial branch of the government and the legislative branch has henceforth been more peaceful.

31 Election of Judges and Magistrates

In South Carolina, members of the supreme court, members of the court of appeals, circuit court judges, family court judges and administrative law judges are elected at a joint meeting of the S.C. House of Representatives and the S.C. Senate. There are five members of the supreme court, nine members of the court of appeals, 46 circuit court judges, 51 family court judges and six administrative law judges. This means that members of the legislature elect a total of 117 judges who perform most of the work of the judiciary. Certainly they perform the most important part of the judiciary's work. Probate judges are elected by popular vote in the general election. Magistrates are appointed by the governor with the advice and consent of the senate.

As long as I can remember, a substantial segment of the populace has sought other ways to elect members of these courts. No serious effort has been made to change the method of electing federal court judges, in spite of the fact that they are perpetually criticized. They are appointed by the President of the United States with the advice and consent of the U.S. Senate, meaning that for most practical purposes the senators name the federal judges.

The time came when it was not possible for members of the general assembly to learn enough to make informed decisions about the many judges they had to elect. In 1997, a constitutional amendment was approved whereby applicants for judgeships must be screened by the Judicial Merit Selection Commission. This amendment sets forth qualifications and permits the commission to qualify and recommend three candidates for each position. It further provided that a member of the legislature could not be elected unless that member first resigned and was out of office for a period of time established by statute. In my opinion, this system has worked satisfactorily since 1997.

While the constitution definitely gave to the governor the authority to appoint magistrates with the advice and consent of the senate, eventually many of the senators simply did not want that chore. For every magistrate appointed, several candidates got mad at the senator. So for many counties, a law was passed providing that those who wished to be magistrates would have to be voted on in the general election. This relieved the senators of the chore and for all practical purposes bound the governor to make the appointment. The appointment was made not because of the judgment of the governor or the senator, but by the will of the voters.

In 1979, the attorney general brought an action in the original jurisdiction of the supreme court challenging the constitutionality of all the statutes requiring candidates for magistrate to be voted on by the people. The supreme court agreed with the attorney general and, accordingly, magistrates are now chosen by the governor subject to approval by the senate. The governor well knows, however, that if he does not appoint the local senator's choice, there will be no advice and consent. Some believe that all judges ought to be elected by the people. I am of the opinion that this is the worst way to elect judges. There is no good way. Certainly, there is no perfect way, but election is the worst way.

32 The Judiciary and the Bar

The work of judges and that of members of the bar is markedly different, but a history of the judiciary would not be complete without a recitation of the relationship between members of the bar and bench. Typically, judges attend conventions of the bar, but members of the bar do not attend judges' meetings. The bar as we now know it, or its forerunner, was formed on November 27, 1884, by 47 lawyers who gathered in Columbia for an organizational meeting. Thirty-four counties were represented and the purpose of the meeting was declared as follows: "The Association is formed to maintain the honor, dignity, and courtesy of the profession of the law; to advance the science of jurisprudence; to promote the due administration of justice, and reforms in the law; to encourage liberal education for the Bar; and to cultivate cordial intercourse among the members of the South Carolina Bar." The S.C. Bar Association was a voluntary organization that functioned until 1975. It had no governmental standing. While serious topics were addressed at the yearly conventions and some learning programs were promulgated, a fair summary of this organization's activities would be considered purely social. In the scheme of things, defense lawyers and corporate counsel dominated the organization.

In 1967, the legislature granted to the Supreme Court of South Carolina the authority to promulgate rules and regulations relative to the practice of law, but such authority was limited. For many years, many lawyers thought the bar should be integrated. Integration would require all practicing attorneys to be members and subject to control by the supreme court. And so from 1884 until 1968, the only organization of South Carolina attorneys was the S.C. Bar Association. In 1967, the legislature authorized the supreme court to promulgate rules "... governing an association to be known as the S.C. Bar which shall be composed of attorneys-at-law of the State, and which shall act as an administrative agent of the Supreme Court for the purpose of improving the administration of justice. ..." The court was also authorized to fix license fees.

On December 14, 1967, the supreme court issued its order establishing the state bar effective March 14, 1968. The court named officers and board members for the first two years, but after that the state bar was to become self-perpetuating. The first president was David W. Robinson, a lifetime advocate of the integrated bar; John M. Spratt of York was the first vice-president. For seven years the state had both the S.C. Bar Association and the S.C. State Bar. As a practical matter, both could not continue. In 1975, the bars approved a merger. The board of governors of each group recommended that the S.C. Bar Association be phased out and that all activities be continued in the name of a mandatory S.C. Bar. The word "state" was dropped from the name. Claude M. Scarborough was elected the first president and Louis Howell of Spartanburg the first vice-president, succeeding Scarborough as president the following year.

Article V of the State Constitution, approved by the people in the fall of 1972 and ratified in the spring of 1973, gave control of the bar to the supreme court in verbiage as follows: "The Supreme Court shall have jurisdiction over the admission to the practice of law and the discipline of persons admitted." Accordingly, statutes no longer control bar activities.

The court and the bar, working together, have carried on many programs of tremendous benefit in the administration of justice, including the S.C. Bar Foundation, clients' security fund, mandatory continuing legal education for attorneys and judges, a "Bridge the Gap" program, and the interest on lawyer trust accounts program. The bench and bar have done much to improve the administration of justice.

The bar has experienced phenomenal growth since 1930. In 1941, 1,200 lawyers practiced in the state. The number increased to 1,300 by 1952 and to 4,000 by 1978. In 1986, more than 6,000 lawyers were licensed to practice. It is my understanding that today the number is approximately 12,000, but only about 9,000 are engaged in day-to-day law practice. The University of South Carolina School of Law's student body is composed of about 750 students. Well over 200 are graduated and admitted to practice in this state each year.

Many contend that the state has more lawyers than it needs and can support. Law schools determine the flow. While the supreme court controls admissions, a quota has never been established. The court has never undertaken to determine the number of persons who should practice law. It only determines competency to practice and admits or refuses to admit based on each applicant's qualifications.

33 Appellate Arbitration

By 1984, the newly created court of appeals was a year old. The two appellate courts were hearing appeals filed approximately two years previously. In order to assist with the backlog, the supreme court passed an order in 1984 permitting appellants and appellees to arbitrate in lieu of appealing in the conventional fashion. Upon receipt of an intention to appeal, the clerk of the supreme court would send to the parties involved a copy of our order. For some time, this system was very productive. The procedure, in lieu of an actual appeal, assured prompt disposition of the case. The arbitrators were directed to file a ruling within 15 days and did not have to write an opinion; instead they merely affirmed, reversed, modified or remanded. This process was cost effective because neither the record nor the briefs had to be printed. All parties had the benefit of a review by three neutral persons without the cost and delay experienced by appealing in the conventional fashion. It is my understanding that Chief Justice Ness discontinued the practice of sending a copy of the order to the parties. In recent years, this order and the rule it inspired have not been very productive.

When the appellate court rules were adopted, the court's order with minor refinements was included and is still in effect as Rule 223. It provides in part as follows: Rule 223. Arbitration of Appeals "(a) Arbitration by Consent. Except criminal cases and civil cases in which the State or one of its political subdivisions is a party, the parties may agree to arbitration of the appeal in lieu of having the case decided by an appellate court. Before any case may be disposed of by arbitration, counsel for all litigants must agree in writing to disposition of the case in that manner. The arbitration panel shall consist of three (3) retired justices, retired judges, active or retired attorneys, or a combination thereof who shall consent in writing to serve. The parties shall select their own arbitrators. The parties agreeing to submit their appeal to arbitration shall file a completed consent to arbitration form supplied by the Clerk of the Supreme Court. Each arbitrator shall receive actual expenses and compensation in the amount of $150 for each case acted upon, to be charged against the losing party."

Under this rule, the supreme court gives the decision of the arbitrators the same weight and force as a directive from the supreme court, and judgment can be entered accordingly. Commenting upon the appellate arbitration rule, Jef Feeley, writing in the *National Law Journal,* said: "The South Carolina Supreme Court is beginning what may be the nation's first binding-arbitration program to be tried at an appellate level." Unfortunately, only a few lawyers are aware of this rule, and those who are aware more often chose not to use it.

34 The Supreme Court's Unusual Chore

A great portion of the work of the supreme court is routine. Normally, the court is asked to determine whether a litigant, civil or criminal, received a fair trial at the circuit court. Occasionally, however, there arises an unusual situation with which the court must become involved. Such a matter arose incident to the election of governor in 1974.

Charles D. "Pug" Ravenel was born in Charleston in 1938. He resided there with his parents until he graduated from high school in 1956. Thereafter, he was away from South Carolina, attending college at Harvard and being employed in New York and/or Washington, for a period of 17 years. He returned to take up residency again in Charleston on March 20, 1972. In 1974, he entered the race for governor, seeking the Democratic nomination.

The Constitution of South Carolina, Article IV, Section 2, provides as follows: "No person shall be eligible to the office of governor who ... shall not have been ... a citizen and resident of this state for five years next preceding the day of election." As the Democratic party primary campaign waxed along, it came to be rumored that Ravenel was not eligible to serve. In order to combat the rumor, he commenced an action in the Court of Common Pleas for Richland County in March 1974, wherein only the Democratic party was named his adversary. He procured an order of the trial court, which was not appealed, permitting him to participate in the Democratic primary. The action was for all practical purposes uncontested. Pug Ravenel was an impressive salesperson, most particularly on television. To the surprise of many, he was victorious in the primary and named the Democratic candidate to oppose all comers in the November general election.

The issue of his eligibility then became crucial. Under law, one may not, even if elected, serve if ineligible under the terms of the constitution. Attorney Eugene Griffith of Newberry brought a class action on behalf of citizens Ben K. Dekle and Milton J. Dukes against the Democratic party and the election commission, asking the court of common pleas to declare Ravenel ineligible. Soon thereafter, Ravenel petitioned the supreme court to assume original jurisdiction to decide the issue. The two actions were consolidated. They came to be heard in the supreme court after Circuit Court Judge J.B. Ness was assigned to take testimony and make an evidentiary record.

The evidence revealed that Ravenel had been away from South Carolina for 17 years prior to 1972. This was documented by his New York income tax returns, his proof of voting in New York, and his resident club memberships. It was basically his contention that only a temporary absence was involved and that he intended in the final analysis to return to South Carolina. The court held that Ravenel was not eligible to serve, which caused pandemonium within the Democratic party. The party was left without a candidate with the November general election fast approaching. Another primary was not practical or possible. That's when the executive committee of the Democratic party designated William Jennings Bryan Dorn as its candidate. Dorn had served in the S.C. House of Representatives, S.C. Senate and in the U.S. Congress for many years. He sought the U.S. Senate nomination in 1948 and was the logical candidate.

James Edwards, the Republican candidate, was elected and became the first Republican governor in South Carolina in many generations. The court over the years has addressed election problems, but I find no history of the court having been involved in the eligibility of one to serve as governor.

35 Supreme Court Turns Cert

Until the 1970s, it was easily possible for the Supreme Court of South Carolina, composed of one panel of five judges, to receive and issue opinions for each of the appeals being filed from year to year. This was true even though in South Carolina any litigant who felt that he or she did not receive a fair trial at the local courthouse level could appeal as a matter of right. In many states, and in the Supreme Court of the United States, appeals were received and acted upon only after a showing had been made. Most courts turned down as many appeals as they accepted.

After it became less expensive to appeal, and after the Supreme Court of the United States held that an indigent litigant was entitled to an appeal without paying the incident costs, appeals escalated. In the late 1970s, the workload of the state supreme court became over-burdensome. The delays incident to the appeals became intolerable. As a result, the legislature, by statute and then constitutionally, created the court of appeals composed of six judges who sat in panels of three. Later, the court of six was expanded to a court of nine.

The number of appeals continued to escalate. For several years, all appeals were filed with the supreme court. That court in turn would transfer a multitude of cases to the court of appeals. The court of appeals could hear any case except those involving death sentences, utility rates, serious constitutional questions, bond obligations, elections, abortions and limitation of state grand jury investigations. Opinions filed by the court of appeals could not automatically be appealed to the supreme court. They could only be appealed after an application for *certiorari*.

In 1999, the Supreme Court of South Carolina became a *cert* court. The legislature passed an act directing that all appeals in which the court of appeals had jurisdiction be filed with the clerk of the court of appeals. This has lessened the work of the supreme court to some degree, but an application for cert need be accompanied by only a minimal fee, and so the supreme court, even though now cert, reviews a tremendous number of applications.

36 The South Carolina Court of Appeals*

People who claim that ours is a litigious society are correct. There has been a tremendous increase in the workload of all courts, and this is especially true of the appeals that have been coming to the Supreme Court of South Carolina. This court, consisting of five justices sitting as one panel, became entirely inadequate in the late 1970s to expedite appeals in a timely manner. It became routine that appeals were heard in the supreme court more than two years after being filed. The general assembly, recognizing the problem, created the court of appeals in 1979. The statute provided for a chief judge and four associate judges to be elected by the general assembly. It also specified the jurisdiction of the court for the purpose of appeals. It was to become effective July 1, 1980.

In late 1979, the attorney general brought an action in the original jurisdiction of the supreme court to test the constitutionality of the act. Several sections of the statute creating the appeals court were declared unconstitutional. During its 1979 session and anticipating the activation of the court, the general assembly elected a chief judge and four associate judges. They were Senator John Martin of Winnsboro, who was named chief judge; Senators Robert Lake of Newberry and Theo Mitchell of Greenville; House Member Thomas Hughston of Greenwood; and former House Member John Gardner of Darlington. The action contested the eligibility of Martin, Mitchell, Lake and Hughston to serve. The act creating the court had attempted to avoid the impact of a 1937 statute that prohibited members of the general assembly from assuming offices created during the term of office for which they were elected. All except Gardner were members of the general assembly when the statute creating the court was passed. The 1937 statute read as follows: "No Senator or Representative shall, during the time for which he was elected, be elected by the General Assembly or appointed by any executive authority to any civil office under the dominion of this State which shall have been created during the time for which such Senator or Representative was elected to serve in the General Assembly."

The statute creating the new court set forth the eligibility requirements of members of the court and attempted (unsuccessfully) to avoid the 1937 statute by including the following:

"Notwithstanding any other provision of law, candidates who meet the [eligibility] requirements as set forth in this section shall be deemed eligible for the office of judge."

The attorney general submitted that this provision was in violation of Article III, Subsection 34, Subdivision 9 of the S.C. Constitution. This subdivision prohibits a special law when a general law can be made applicable. The supreme court held that the attorney general was correct. The effect of this ruling was to leave in office only one judge, John Gardner. The assembly might have overcome this problem by simply repealing the 1937 statute, but that was never attempted. This opinion chilled the enthusiasm of the legislature to take action that would activate the appeals court. It declined to elect eligible judges to fill the four vacancies and failed to provide any appropriation to implement the act, although the supreme court held that the appeals court was constitutionally created. In the absence of an additional appellate court, the caseload in the Supreme Court of South Carolina continued to escalate.

Finally, in 1983, the statute that created the court of appeals was substantially amended. The amendment called for a chief judge and five associate judges who would sit in panels of three. It gave to the court jurisdiction to hear appeals, except in cases that involved the death penalty, utility rates, significant constitutional questions, bond issues and election contests. Judges were elected and court began operation in the fall of 1983. Those chosen to serve were Chief Judge Alexander Sanders, Judges John Gardner, Curtis Shaw, Randy Bell, Jasper Cureton and C. Tolbert Goolsby.

Along with the statutes creating and recreating or activating the court of appeals, the general assembly proposed by joint resolution a constitutional amendment giving it constitutional status. The people approved the amendment in November 1984 and the legislature ratified the amendment early in 1985. It is interesting to note that Senators Martin, Lake and Mitchell and Representative Hughston did not seek the office, even though they would have been eligible to serve, given that they were in a new term of office. Sanders had previously served in the assembly, as had Gardner. Shaw, Bell, Cureton and Goolsby had no legislative experience.

The court of appeals is not a court of last resort: that is the purview of the supreme court. Persons who are unhappy with the court of appeals' rulings may petition the supreme court for a writ of *certiorari*, and many do. It is, however, the consensus of thinking among both judges and lawyers that the court of appeals must not be merely one more echelon of appeal and delay. While many applications for writs are filed with the Supreme Court of South Carolina, few are granted.

In the creation of the court of appeals, South Carolina joined about 40 other states that have an intermediate appellate court. In 1995, the legislature amended the statute so as to add three additional judges to the court of appeals. The court continues to serve in panels of three, and occasionally an *en banc* session is held.

Members of the S.C. Court of Appeals who served since the offices were created in 1987:

Alex Sanders Jr., C.J.	William L. Howard
Randall Bell	H. Samuel Stilwell
Jasper Cureton	Ralph K. Anderson
John Gardner	Thomas E. Huff
Tolbert Goolsby Jr.	Donald W. Beatty
Curtis Shaw	Bruce Williams
William T. Howell, C.J.	Malcombe D. Shuler
Carol Connor	John W. Kittredge
Kaye G. Hearn, C.J.	

*Adapted from *Littlejohn's Half Century at the Bench and Bar (1936–1986)*.

37 Master-in-Equity Courts

It appears that the office of master-in-equity has existed in South Carolina since colonial times, having its origin in the English courts of Chancery. Several acts from 1746 to 1846 defined and redefined the office. The South Carolina Constitution of 1868 provided for the merger of the courts of law and equity. Also, the circuit court was established, which was divided into the S.C. Court of General Sessions and the S.C. Court of Common Pleas.

From 1868 until 1973, there were many acts relating to the office of the master-in-equity. Some of the acts actually abolished the office, resulting in a return to the referee system. During this time, the masters as well as the referees would hear cases that were referred from a circuit court judge. At the conclusion of the hearing, the master or referee would forward a report to the referring circuit court judge. If the report were not contested, an order would be signed by the circuit court judge according to the report of the master or referee. If a party were not satisfied with the ruling of the circuit court judge based on the report, an appeal could be filed with the Supreme Court of South Carolina.

In 1973, the S.C. General Assembly ratified Article V of the S.C. Constitution, which created the unified judicial system. This system consisted of the Supreme Court of South Carolina, the S.C. Circuit Court and other courts of uniform jurisdiction that might be established by general law. In 1976, it appeared that the office of the master-in-equity would be abolished effective July 1, 1979, pursuant to the enactment of Act 690. The governor signed Act 164 on July 16, 1979, which incorporated the office of the master-in-equity into the uniform judicial system. Pursuant to Act 164, the masters were authorized to enter final orders instead of the reports that would have to be confirmed by the circuit court. Also, for the first time, the parties to the action could agree that an appeal from a master's order would be to the Supreme Court of South Carolina.

Rule 53 of the South Carolina Rules of Civil Procedure, which deals with the authority of the masters, now provides that in "an action where the consent, in a default case or an action for foreclosure, some or all of the causes of action may be referred to a master… In all other actions, the circuit court may upon motion of any party or on its own motion, direct a reference of some or all of the causes of action in a case." Once a matter is referred, the master shall "exercise all power and authority which a circuit judge sitting without a jury would have in a similar matter." Finally, "an appeal from the master's order will be to the Supreme Court or the Court of Appeals pursuant to the South Carolina Appellate Court Rules." These changes to the rules relating to masters were adopted to create uniformity since the masters became part of the unified judicial system.

A master-in-equity no longer has to seek office in a general election. An applicant for the office must be at least 32 years of age, have practiced law for at least eight years, be a resident of South Carolina for at least five years and found to be qualified by the S.C. Judicial Merit Selection Commission. After completing the required background investigations and judicial screening, the master is appointed for a term of six years by the governor with the advice and consent of the general assembly. The master-in-equity may be full time or part time, and is compensated by the county governing body. As of 2004, there were 22 masters-in-equity serving counties with populations of 130,000 or more. Full-time masters are not permitted to practice law, but part-time masters may. Salaries of the master-in-equity are standardized with full-time masters, who are paid a percentage of a circuit court judge's salary based on the population of the county that the master serves. Master's salaries are paid by their respective counties. The work and jurisdiction of the master-in-equity has changed over the years and now, with their incorporation into the unified court system, they have come to play an important part in the administration of justice in South Carolina.

38 Probate Courts

Judges of the probate courts in all 46 counties of South Carolina are elected in a general election. The judges need not be members of the bar, but they are in most of the larger counties. The work of the probate court is becoming more important because people are dying with larger estates to be distributed. These courts are a part of the unified judicial system.

In 1983, the probate courts began to be monitored by the S.C. Court Administration, an arm of the supreme court. Until that time, all probate courts operated under individual systems for numbering estates and guardian files, or packages, as some courts called them. Once court administration began monitoring, the file numbering systems were mandated and made uniform across the state. Prior to court administration's involvement, many old estates never closed, but probate court must now report monthly the status of every estate. For those estates that have remained open longer than one year, a reason must be supplied for the estate's failure to close.

For many years, the bench and bar have appreciated the fact that there ought to be a South Carolina probate code. Soon after retiring as supreme court justice, Lionel Legge was assigned the chore of coming up with a probate code to be submitted to the general assembly. Nothing came of his recommendations. It was not until 1986 that the Probate Code of South Carolina was finally agreed upon and adopted by the general assembly to become effective July 1, 1987.

The code gave the probate court the added duty and authority to supervise and hear contests relative to trusts. This is one of the more important changes brought about by the new code. This code also gave litigants the right to a jury trial, a right seldom used at the probate court level. More often the probate judge, either with or without the consent of the litigants, refers the cases to the circuit court for jury trial. All rulings of the probate judge are subject to appeal to the circuit courts, but the parties may agree to have the appeal from the probate court go to the Supreme Court of South Carolina. The new code changed the designation of "executor" to that of "personal representative." The probate courts continue to issue marriage licenses and to perform many marriage ceremonies. Historically, wills required the signature of three witnesses. Upon the death of the testator, it was oftentimes difficult to find all of the witnesses to go to the probate court and testify that this was truly the will of the testator. In more recent times, only two witnesses are required and the wills may now be made self-proving.

In 2004–2005, a singular honor came to Raymond Eubanks, judge of probate for Spartanburg County. He was elected president of the National College of Probate Judges. In 2005, he retired after 25 years of service and the governor appointed Ponda Caldwell, who had worked in that office for 27 years, the new probate judge. She was promptly confirmed by the S.C. Senate.

39 Lawyer Competency

The supreme court has endeavored to see that only truly competent persons practice law in South Carolina. At the same time, lawyers have done much to improve their skills in the trial of cases and other legal undertakings. The S.C. Bar Association was formed in 1884 by 47 lawyers who gathered in Columbia for an organizational meeting. There were 34 counties at that time and all of them were represented. Given its primary function as a social organization until 1975, the bar association was purely voluntary. In large measure, defense lawyers and corporate counsel dominated its activities. It operated independent of any control by the court, the legislature or any other governmental entity. In 1967, the legislature granted to the supreme court the authority to promulgate rules and regulations relative to the practice of law, but such authority was limited.

For several years, leading members of the S.C. Bar Association advocated an integrated bar under which all practicing lawyers in South Carolina would be required to participate as members. It was not until 1967 that the legislature gave to the supreme court the authority to bring about an integrated bar, which we have had since 1968. The Act of 1967 authorized the supreme court to promulgate rules "…governing an association to be known as the South Carolina Bar which shall be composed of the attorneys at law of the state, and which shall act as an administrative agency of the Supreme Court of South Carolina for the purpose of improving the administration of justice."

In 1967, the supreme court issued an order that established the S.C. State Bar, effective March 14, 1968, exiting along side the voluntary S.C. Bar Association. Both organizations continued to operate separately until January 31, 1975, when the two merged. The board of governors of each group recommended that the voluntary South Carolina Bar Association be phased out and that all activities be continued in the name of the mandated S.C. Bar.

Article V of the State Constitution, approved by the people in the fall of 1972 and ratified by the legislature in the spring of 1973, gave control of the bar to the supreme court as follows: "The Supreme Court shall have jurisdiction over the admission to the practice of law and the discipline of persons admitted." Legislative statutes controlling bar matters thereupon became void.

In addition to the programs established by the court and the bar, the University of South Carolina School of Law has also made an important contribution, improving its curriculum by requiring more practical studies, for example. Because the school now receives four or five applications for each freshman it can admit, the school can be more selective. At the time of this writing, the law school had about 750 students. It accepts approximately 250 students every year. We will watch with interest the new law school in Charleston, which began operation in September 2004.

Lawyers who represent mostly plaintiffs have formed the S.C. Trial Lawyers Association. This group meets annually, usually at Hilton Head, and conducts some of the most beneficial programs that have ever come to my attention. This group is active in legislative matters and usually takes a great deal of interest in the election of judges. Similarly, those who represent defendants also have an organization called the S.C. Defense Lawyers Organization. This group conducts excellent programs designed to hone the skills of its members. Members of the bar, as well as judges working together, have done much to improve the administration of justice in South Carolina.

40 Specialization in South Carolina

Judges and lawyers from throughout the United States have shown considerable interest in the progress made at the bench and bar in South Carolina in the field of improving lawyer competency. A special interest has been indicated in the fact that we have, in a comparatively short period of time, put our specialization program into orbit. Courts and bar associations in other states recently have been wrestling with this matter and have been making progress in varying degrees – but slowly.

The approach to the problem of specialization depends largely upon the constitutional and statutory law of the state involved. In South Carolina, the chore has been somewhat simplified by the fact that our state constitution gives to the supreme court "…jurisdiction over the admission to the practice of law and the discipline of persons admitted." Accordingly, full authority is vested in the high court to determine not only the qualifications of applicants but the prerequisites for remaining competent so long as one practices law.

Appreciating the groundswell for the improvement of lawyer competency (spoken of often by former Chief Justice Warren E. Burger), our court has taken several actions designed to improve legal education over and above the specialization program. Among the programs that have been initiated recently, and which are serving the bench and bar well, are requirements that practicing attorneys participate in 12 hours of continuing legal education annually, that judges attend continuing judicial education programs, and that applicants to the bar undergo a "Bridge the Gap" program. In addition, a student practice rule has been promulgated and applicants are required to have studied in certain important areas of the law sometimes referred to as the "reading, 'riting and 'rithmetic of the law." Each admittee to the bar must have 11 trial experiences before coming to try a case alone.

In South Carolina, the bench and bar have realized that lawyers must keep abreast of what is new if they are to serve their clients well. The S.C. Bar, the S.C. Trial Lawyers Association (a plaintiffs' group) and the S.C. Defense Trial Attorneys' Association (a defendants' group) have programs regularly which qualify for court requirements. In addition, programs are inaugurated regularly by the competency commission and held at the University of South Carolina School of Law. Seminars are held on many subjects giving attorneys varied choices. Any specialty group may seek recognition of its own legal education specialty program by the Commission on Continuing Legal Education. Many attorneys receive more than the 12 hours required, averaging 16 hours per year.

Several years ago members of the Supreme Court of South Carolina reached the conclusion that the law has become so massive that no one attorney can be good in all fields. Laypeople in pursuit of a lawyer should have some means of determining which attorneys are qualified to handle a particular case. This is especially true since the Supreme Court of the United States held that lawyers may extol their own virtues by advertising. If a lawyer may advertise, the question immediately arises: What representation should he be able to make relative to his competency?

One of the big problems relative to any specialization program is the matter of certification. Who shall approve and designate the specialist? Under our constitution there is no question that the supreme court must be the final certifying authority. For several years prior to the Supreme Court of South Carolina's certification rule number 53, continuing legal education had been mandated. The bar accepted the requirement rather gracefully after "grandfathering" all attorneys who had practiced more than 30 years. This killed off the older lawyers' lobby against the rule. The bar also supports our specialization program and readily accepts our mandatory continuing legal education.

In order to bring the specialization program into being, the court, working with the S.C. Bar, appointed a commission on continuing lawyer competency. In addition to overseeing the lawyer's mandatory legal education requirement, it also supervises the certification program. The court has the full cooperation of the bar. The House of Delegates submits a list of nominees for the commission from which the court chooses 10. This commission is authorized to select fields of specialization and to appoint specialization advisory boards to recommend standards and procedures for certification within the respective specialties.

When it designates a new specialty field or defines the scope of the practice of a new specialty, the commission operates at its own initiative or upon petition of 100 members of the bar. An advisory board is answerable to the commission, and the commission in turn is answerable to the supreme court. As of this time, (1) taxation law, (2) estate planning and probate law and (3) employment and labor law are specialty fields already approved. The family law practice was at one time approved by the supreme court, but the approval was later revoked before it was actually in operation.

The court may set minimum standards for specialist certification. The standards will, of course, vary from specialty to specialty. Membership in the S.C. Bar is always required. An application must be filed giving information that in the view of the commission entitles the applicant to advertise himself as a specialist in the particular field. Usually five years practice of the law is required and a showing must be made of substantial involvement in the practice of law in the specialty field for which application is made.

Certification in a particular field does not limit the specialist from a general practice. Renewal of certification is required every five years. Any lawyer who is refused certification or renewal or whose certification is revoked has the right to a hearing before a specialization advisory board and the right to appeal to the commission as well as the right to a judicial review by the court.

The number of attorneys certified within the three specialties already established is growing. New specialties, such as real estate law, are being considered. There is general approval of our overall lawyer competency improvement programs including the specialization program. The support comes not only from lawyers and judges but from the public as well. It serves the public by helping those in need of representation choose a competent lawyer for a particular case. We are complimented that members of the bench and bar from other states have sought information from our competency commission and are emulating our program.

41 Judges and Politics

In some states, there has been a tendency for members of the judiciary to use the office as a steppingstone to a governorship, a position in the U.S. Senate or some other high office. In South Carolina this has not been the case, but with a few exceptions. In 1912, Chief Justice Ira Jones resigned his office in order to run for governor against the incumbent Cole Blease. Jones was not successful and did not seek other public office. In 1938, J. Strom Thurmond was elected circuit judge of the Eleventh Judicial Circuit. He served in that capacity until World War II when he left the office in order to enter the U.S. Army. At that time the law provided that if a person left employment to serve in the United States armed forces the employer was required to give the job back upon return from service. Accordingly, the legislature left the Thurmond judgeship vacant until his return from the war in 1946.

Thurmond continued to serve as judge for several months and then resigned to enter the race for governor of South Carolina. There were 10 candidates seeking the office that year. At that time, the Democratic party primary was the equivalent of the final election since the Republication party presence had not yet strengthened. Dr. James M. McLeod of Florence and Thurmond ran a second race, and Thurmond won. He served as governor until January of 1951.

In the fall of 1950, Thurmond sought to unseat U.S. Senator Olin D. Johnston, but was not successful. Having been defeated, many people were of the opinion that Thurmond's political career was at an end. He returned to Aiken and entered the practice of law with Charles E. Simons, who was later made a U.S. District Court judge.

In 1942, Eugene Blease, who had retired as chief justice of the Supreme Court of South Carolina, was a candidate for the U.S. Senate opposing Burnett R. Maybank, who was running for reelection. Blease was almost successful but did not win. In 1986, Circuit Court Judge Frank Eppes, who had served as a circuit judge for more than a quarter of a century, resigned in order to seek the office of governor. He was not successful in this undertaking and chose to continue to serve as a circuit court judge by special appointment of several chief justices. In recent years, Marion Kinon, after retiring as a circuit court judge, was elected and served as a member of the S.C. House of Representatives from Dillon County. About the same time, Lawrence Richter, after having served as a circuit court judge, was elected to the S.C. Senate.

Those who were of the opinion that the political career of Judge/Governor Thurmond was over following his 1950 defeat were badly mistaken. In 1954, the office of U.S. Senator from South Carolina was up for grabs. Senator Burnett Maybank was running in the Democratic primary (equivalent to election) unopposed. On September 1, 1954, Maybank died of a massive heart attack.

The S.C. Democratic Executive Committee called a hurried meeting and designated S.C. Senator Edgar Brown of Barnwell to be the Democratic nominee in the upcoming November general election. Brown had served as speaker of the house, as a member of the S.C. Senate and as head of the Democratic party for many years. He was popular and unbeatable in his own county of Barnwell, but he was not as popular throughout the rest of the state.

Thurmond, who had always had his political ear to the ground, sensed that the people did not want Edgar Brown to represent them in the U.S. Senate. The former judge/governor undertook a write-in candidacy and defeated the Democratic nominee by approximately 60,000 votes. To my recollection, he is the only judge who has been successful in a political campaign for higher office after having left the judiciary. Until the 1960s and '70s, nomination on the Democratic ticket was the equivalent of election. In 1964, Thurmond switched parties and became a Republican. He had the distinction of being elected to the U.S. Senate on a write-in vote, as an Independent, as a Democrat and as a Republican. Thurmond served 48 years and then retired. He died at the age of 100 in 2004. With these exceptions, the judges of South Carolina have little concerned themselves with running for elective office.

42 Judges and the University of South Carolina School of Law

Nearly all of the judges serving today on the supreme court, the circuit courts and in the family courts of this state are graduates of the University of South Carolina School of Law.

In days past, one could be admitted to the bar and, in turn, serve as a justice or a judge of the courts of record by studying law for two years in the office of an established attorney and by standing a state bar examination. One could also become an attorney and/or judge in this state by reason of the rule of comity, by which a lawyer who had practiced law for three years in another state could be automatically admitted to the S.C. Bar. These methods are no longer available.

Until 1921, there was no other school of law in South Carolina. The law school at the University of South Carolina was accredited by the American Bar Association in 1925 and became a member of the Association of American Law Schools about the same time. In 1921, there was established at Furman University in Greenville a law school. It survived until 1932. John Plyer was the dean and later came to serve as judge of the Greenville County Court. There simply were not enough students to warrant Furman's new undertaking. In 1947, there was established a law school at the South Carolina State College in Orangeburg that survived until 1966. It was designed to serve black students, but the number of students did not warrant the school's effort. About that time, the University of South Carolina School of Law began admitting blacks.

From 1966 until 2004, there was only one law school in South Carolina. In 2004, under the guidance and promotion of former Chief Judge Alex Sanders of the S.C. Court of Appeals, there was established the Law School at Charleston. As of this writing, the school had admitted about 125 freshmen and turned down about 800 applicants.

Most, if not all, of the academic schools in South Carolina have graduated students who ended up at the University of South Carolina School of Law and later became judges. At this time, Wofford College boasts of having three of the five members of the Supreme Court of South Carolina graduates of its institution. They are sometimes referred to in good humor as the "Wofford Mafia." Wofford has also supplied a lion's share of the circuit court judges and family court judges in this state.

During the depression years of the 1930s, it was not difficult to gain admission to the University of South Carolina School of Law. My class consisted of 33 students, only 18 of whom graduated, and only six of whom survive as of 2004.

There is substantial debate as to whether South Carolina needs an additional law school. We will have to wait and examine the quality of its graduates. If the Charleston school provides as good or better lawyers than the University of South Carolina School of Law, we will say it was a good thing. If it does not it, like some of the other law schools once established in the state, may not survive.

43 Prayer In Court*

When I came to the bar in 1936, it was not unusual for circuit court judges to open court on Monday morning with prayer by a local minister. This was particularly true in criminal court. Not all of the judges followed the custom, but several regularly advised the clerk of court in advance to have a preacher available. Nowadays, the custom is seldom followed, but occasionally some judges still arrange for the opening of circuit court with prayer.

At a term of criminal court in Aiken, Judge Frank Eppes of Greenville realized that no arrangement had been made for the services of a local minister and inquired if there might be a local preacher in the audience. One promptly volunteered and proceeded to give the invocation on behalf of the court. Judge Eppes was greatly embarrassed to learn a little bit later that this praying man was a defendant in the criminal court beginning that same day. Upon gaining this knowledge, Eppes continued this man's case to another term so that the state's case might not be prejudiced by having this defendant call upon the Lord prior to calling upon the jury.

When I first became an associate justice of the supreme court in 1967, we followed the same practice. At each meeting of the court on Monday morning, a pastor would open court with prayer. A modest honorarium ($20, if I am not mistaken) was provided by the legislature for the invited minister. Over the years, it appeared to become a little more difficult to arrange opening court in this manner, and the custom trickled out of the supreme court procedures.

Actually, it never occurred to me that such a custom was even debatably unconstitutional. The issue was raised in 1982 in the case of *The United States v. Walker*. It appears that U.S. District Court Judge Solomon Blatt Jr. opened a term of criminal court in Charleston with prayer by a local minister. Upon appeal to the Fourth Circuit Court sitting in Richmond, counsel for a convicted defendant submitted as a basis for a new trial that church and state had been wrongfully intermingled. The prayer was not recorded, but apparently there was a reference to the shooting of President Ronald Reagan, which had occurred a week earlier. The preacher requested God's assistance in guiding the jury to do what was right. At the end of the prayer, counsel objected and sought a mistrial.

Commenting upon the issue raised, Judge Clement Haynesworth, writing for the court, said: "The practice, however, is a needlessly risky one. Because each minister composes his own prayer, its content is beyond the control of the judge. A minister, knowing little of the ground rules for jury trials, may inadvertently say something that is prejudicial to a defendant. We may assume that they are persons of discretion, but a court is not a church, and things that may be said with discretion and appropriateness in a church may be indiscreet or inappropriate in a courtroom."

I have never followed the practice of opening court with prayer, but I have participated on many occasions where the custom was adhered to in a particular county, without ever thinking that there could conceivably be any objection under the First, Sixth or Fourteenth Amendment to the Constitution of the United States. The holdings of the Fourth Circuit Court of Appeals are not binding on state courts within that circuit or any other circuit. Until the Supreme Court of the United States indicates a similar view, I would not hesitate to continue the custom. When I held the first term of court in the new Spartanburg County Courthouse in 1958, it was my pleasure to have my Sunday school teacher from the First Baptist Church of Spartanburg participate in the opening session. My teacher brought, on behalf of the class, Bibles for use in both the east and west courtrooms; both Bibles are still in use today. Charles Lea, the teacher, rendered a dedicatory prayer. For many years, thousands of witnesses have placed their left hands on these same Bibles and have sworn (or affirmed) to tell the truth, the whole truth and nothing but the truth. Hopefully, they did. No doubt a whale of a lot of them did not.

While presiding over a term of criminal court in Aiken, Solicitor Leonard A. Williamson came to my chambers and stated that he was about to call a case wherein a citizen was assaulted in the yard of a church. He said that several members of the church would be testifying and that they were religiously opposed to swearing but agreeable to affirming. I told him that it created no problem – I would simply substitute the word "affirm" when administering the oath. The jury found the defendant not guilty. The witnesses had not testified as the solicitor had been led to believe. The solicitor's comment was: "These people are awful. They refused to swear. They promised to affirm and then they lied like hell."

*Adapted from *Littlejohn's Half Century at the Bench and Bar (1936–1986)*.

44 Sentencing Guidelines

Since 1930, and perhaps before, trial judges have received more criticism because of the disparity in criminal sentences than any other single issue. Critics have argued over the years that the severity of a sentence should not depend upon whether Judge Hardknocks or Judge Creampuff happened to be assigned to the court on the day of the conviction or guilty plea.

The circuit court judges, and the supreme court too, have wrestled with this problem for many years and discussed it at many seminars and conferences. Perhaps less has been accomplished in this undertaking than any other issue the judges and justices have discussed. It was first made a topic of serious discussion and consideration at the South Carolina Judicial Conference held in August of 1968. Trial judges admit that sentences should be uniform, and each judge in essence says, "If other judges would pass sentences like mine, there would be complete uniformity." Judges are protective of their discretion.

The constitutions of the United States and of South Carolina guarantee a fair trial to every person accused of a crime. Courts have been meticulous in seeing that this constitutional provision is honored. Only a minimum of time and effort has been devoted to seeing that a defendant once convicted, or who pleads guilty, receives a fair sentence. In an effort to make sentences more uniform, the supreme court appointed a commission chaired by Associate Justice David Harwell to come up with a recommendation hoping to mimic, to some extent, the federal sentencing guidelines. The recommendation was submitted to the general assembly in the form of a "final report summary." Chief Justice George T. Gregory Jr., in his address to the general assembly on February 27, 1991, endorsed the work product of this commission and urged the assembly to look favorably upon its recommendation.

The S.C. General Assembly took no action. Instead, it has been content to enact statutes mandating minimum sentences as related to several serious offenses. Mandatory sentences are severely criticized by some segments of the legal profession because the legislature can take into consideration the nature of the offense but never take into consideration the nature of the defendant involved.

The U.S. Congress was concerned in the 1980s with the fact that sentences were not uniform. It enacted into law what we refer to as "federal guidelines." District court judges, in passing sentences, were bound by a formula set forth in the law. Federal trial judges detested them because the guidelines infringed upon their discretion. Over the years, more and more lawmakers, judges and members of the public became unhappy with the guidelines.

In the early part of 2005, the Supreme Court of the United States put the matter to rest and held, in effect, that the sentencing judges were not bound by the guidelines, but should only consider them in determining sentences for the various offenses. Guidelines were adopted in many state courts but never in South Carolina. Accordingly, disparity in sentences continues to be a problem in all federal and state courts.

45 Rule Making

There has been much rule-making history at the bench and bar since 1930. Until 1985, there were three sources of rules with which an attorney and judge should have been familiar. They were supreme court rules, statutory rules and opinions of the supreme court. No one place existed for lawyers to learn how to try cases.

In 1938, the federal courts adopted the Federal Rules of Civil Procedure. By 1958, 10 of the state courts adopted the federal rules, some with and some without variations. These federal rules were proving most satisfactory.

In 1958, when Chief Justice Taylor Stukes took office, he had the court create the judicial council whose duty it was to study the administration of justice and recommend changes. The council was composed of 21 outstanding lawyers and judges. The chief justice served as chair. The council appointed a committee to study the rules of civil procedure and to report its recommendation to the council. That committee was composed of Judge Bruce Littlejohn as chair, Judge James M. Brailsford Jr., Senator L. Marion Gressette, attorneys David W. Robinson and Ben Scott Whaley. Working with the committee were representatives of the general assembly, namely Senator John Martin, Senator James Morrison, Representatives John D. Lee Jr. and Thomas E. Walsh. Reporters for the committee were professor Charles H. Randall Jr. and attorney Frank K. Sloan. They served the committee well.

The committee on civil procedure held many hearings and came up with a modified version of the Federal Rules of Civil Procedure adapted to South Carolina's needs. The full S.C. Judicial Council approved the recommendation and, on January 30, 1958, the chief justice, as chair of the council, sent the recommendation to the S.C. Senate and to the S.C. House of Representatives.

Judges and lawyers gave great support to the council's recommendation. At that time, the thinking of the bench and bar was that the rules had to be approved by the general assembly. The S.C. House of Representatives approved the rules with little debate and by near-unanimous consent.

The senate was composed in part by elderly lawyers who did not want to be bothered with changes. They were satisfied to practice law as they had all along. By a vote of 20 to 21, with five members absent, the rules were rejected. About that time, committee member David Robinson made the observation that we were ahead of our time. He predicted that the time would come, perhaps in 10 years, when the federal rules would in essence be adopted for use in South Carolina courts. The rules having been rejected, lawyers and judges continued to hold court while searching for cognates in the supreme court rules, statutory rules and other rulings in case law.

Prior to 1968, little discovery was available in the trial of civil cases. A time arrived when the supreme court felt compelled to do something about it. The court adopted a substantial part of the discovery rules to be found in the federal rules. At that time, Senator Marion Gressette had served in the senate for 31 years. He was president *pro tempore* in the senate and chair of the judiciary committee. He wanted no rules other than those adopted by the general assembly. The court was holding its meetings in the supreme court offices in the capitol. The senate was in session upstairs. Gressette sent Lieutenant Governor John West down to the court to ask it to withhold the effective day of the rules until he had a chance to approve them. The court rejected his request, igniting a dispute between the senate judiciary committee and the supreme court that lasted until the death of Senator Gressette in 1984.

During the 1960s and 1970s, there was a litigation explosion in South Carolina – indeed, throughout the United States. More people were suing and more people needed to be sued. The rule-making authority continued to be in debate.

In August 1982, the supreme court saw a need to settle the rule-making authority and issued an order of its own volition, declaring the rule-making authority lay in the supreme court to the exclusion of a legislative blessing. In this order, quite a few procedures were established contrary to statutes and case law. The order, approved by all five members of the supreme court, irritated members of the house and senate – especially the lawyers and, more particularly, Gressette. The order declared in no uncertain terms that the legislature had no right to enact rules of procedure binding the unified court system. It said: "We therefore hold that the judicial power of the court system inherently requires this court to promulgate rules to promote justice and to ensure its administration."

The order went on to invalidate that section of the code which provided that an answer or demurrer must be served within 20 days after the service of a copy of the complaint. It ruled that service of the answer or demurrer must be within 30 days.

The legislature has been slow to give up authority. Because the court had assumed the right to pass rules, the legislature could only change such by a constitutional amendment. The general assembly hastened to propose a constitutional amendment stripping the supreme court of its rule-making authority and vesting it in the general assembly.

I was sworn in and took office on March 7, 1984. Chief Justice Lewis retired on that day and Marion Gressette died the same week. This eliminated the two antagonists. Robert Sheheen was chair of the S.C. House Judiciary Committee. He came to my office at the supreme court and said, in effect, "In our ire we have proposed an amendment to the constitution which is not good for the administration of justice. If the court would agree we would like to withdraw the proposed amendment and propose a substitute whereby the supreme court would make rules and forward them to the house and senate judiciary committees for scrutiny. The house and senate would have 90 days within which to reject the proposed rules, otherwise they would become effective."

I told Chairman Sheheen that I would agree if the members of my court did, but I added, "It is late in the session. There are many bills pending. It would be difficult, if not impossible, for you to withdraw this former proposed amendment and have the new proposed amendment adopted." Bob replied, "I think I can do it and I would like to try."

All members of the court agreed; the members of the general assembly (to my amazement) approved a substitute amendment to the constitution which remains in effect today. The new approach to changing rules has proved satisfactory. Several proposals have been sent to the general assembly and none has been rejected. In my humble opinion, rule-making authority is right where it ought to be. Everyone seems to be satisfied.

After the South Carolina version of the Federal Rules of Civil Procedure was adopted, the legislature approved one bill that repealed approximately 300 statutes that were, in effect, rules of civil procedure. The new rules became effective as of July 1, 1985, 22 days before my retirement. I take much pride in the fact that I was helpful not only in 1958, but also in 1982 and 1985 in changes that improved the administration of justice.

46 Supreme Court Opinions

Because, in days of yore, members of the Supreme Court of South Carolina were only partially employed, they had plenty of time to write scholarly opinions. As late as 1967, when I first joined the court, there were only 151 appeals filed during the entire year. The court continued to write an opinion in every appeal regardless of its importance or whether or not precedence was involved. Not until the 1980s did the number of appeals filed each year escalate, averaging about 200 appeals annually. That number quickly escalated to 1,000 appeals every year, brought about by two dynamics:

First, the court had previously required records and briefs in all appeals to be printed, for which the printer charged $11 per page. This was truly burdensome in a great portion of the cases. The Supreme Court of South Carolina changed the rule so that records and briefs could be reproduced by way of mimeograph or other methods of copy. The cost of appeals, though still not cheap, is not so burdensome as it once was. The reduced cost makes it more feasible to gamble on the result of an appeal.

Second, the Supreme Court of the United States ruled that if a rich man could afford an appeal, the government had to give a poor man an appeal. Accordingly, upon conviction or plea of guilty, a lawyer must now tell his client he has the right to appeal. Knowing it is free, a client will often say in effect, "Of course, I want to appeal. The jury was ignorant; the judge didn't know the law; and my lawyer was incompetent." These two changes in the law caused many more appeals.

In light of the increased appeals, the Supreme Court of South Carolina passed a rule asserting that an opinion would not be filed unless some matter of precedence was involved. This did not reduce reading and research time, but it did cut down considerably on the court's writing time. The court concluded that it was a disservice to the bar and to litigants to publish opinions that established no true precedence. Today, the Supreme Court of South Carolina and the S.C. Court of Appeals are deciding more cases without written opinions than with. The new rule was long overdue.

47 Judge, Associate Justice and Chief Justice Ness

J.B. Ness of Bamberg played an important part in the development of legal education and lawyer competency. After graduating from the University of South Carolina School of Law in 1940, he returned to his hometown of Bamberg and practiced law until 1958 when he was elected circuit court judge of the Second Judicial Circuit composed of Bamberg, Barnwell and Aiken counties. In 1974, he was elected as an associate justice of the Supreme Court of South Carolina. He served in that capacity until July 1985 when he assumed the office of chief justice. He served as chief justice until his 72nd birthday when he was, by law, required to retire. In all of these capacities, he was well known as an innovator, always anxious to try something new that might improve the court system and the administration of justice. As chief justice, he was known for performing many non paying jobs. There are six particularly worthy of note:

(1) While serving as circuit court judge and as a member of the supreme court, Ness developed an excellent trial charge book which was so well received by the bench that copies were distributed to all of the newly elected judges over a period of years.

(2) For many years, Ness was in charge of an orientation program for new judges. The court had decided that newly elected circuit court judges would benefit from an orientation program. At these seminars he attempted to teach the new judges techniques of operating an efficient court – covering such things as docket control, charging the jury, writing orders and many other things with which even the most successful lawyer had no reason to concern himself or herself.

(3) He organized and headed the "Bridge the Gap" program from 1985 until his death in 1991. This program is mandated for all those admitted to the bar. It is designed to assist young lawyers who are about to begin a practice by teaching them what to do when clients start walking into the office and how to conduct themselves properly when in the courtroom for the first time. This type of program is growing in popularity throughout the country.

(4) In August of each year, Ness held a learning seminar for state and federal judges' law clerks, which he personally supervised. It was a great benefit to those who have been employed as clerks and it saved judges a tremendous amount of time orienting their new law clerks.

(5) He was chair of the Judicial Continuing Legal Education Committee. This committee inaugurates, promotes and monitors programs designed to keep the judiciary abreast of what is new at the law.

(6) While attending to all of these chores, Ness found time over a period of years to teach a course at the University of South Carolina School of Law for which he received no compensation. In the classroom he endeavored to teach law students how to try cases.

Notwithstanding the many activities in which he was engaged, he periodically accepted public speaking engagements at schools, civic clubs and other meetings. These lectures have been helpful in educating the populace about what goes on in the judicial world.

Many students graduating from law school sought to serve as his law clerk because they had come to know that associating with him provided supplemental education that the law school was not prepared to supply. Our friend died in 1991, following a fast-moving cancer. I believe that Justice Ness contributed more to lawyer competency and legal education than any other person with whom I have been associated.

48 Growth of Judiciary

From 1930 until 1962, the supreme court, consisting of five members, and the circuit courts, consisting of 14 judges, were sufficient to carry on the state's judicial business, with the help of the magistrates and a few county courts with fewer jurisdictions than the circuit courts and more than the magistrates. Additional circuit court judges were added for the first time in 1962. Since that time it has been necessary to add many circuit court judges, family court judges, members of the court of appeals and administrative law judges. The expansion of the court system is reflected in a chart as follows:

1930   5   Supreme court (chief justice and 4 associate justices)
        14   Circuit court judges
        19   Total

1962   5   Supreme court
        15   Circuit judges (12th circuit divided and
             15th circuit created)
        20   Total

1966   5   Supreme court
        16   Circuit judges (6th circuit and 7th circuit
             divided and 16th circuit created)
        21   Total

1976   5   Supreme court
        25   Circuit judges (9 resident circuit judges added)
        38   Family court judges elected
        68   Total

1977   5   Supreme court
        25   Circuit judges
        44   Family court judges (6 family court judges added)
        74   Total

1978   5   Supreme court
        25   Circuit judges
        46   Family court judges (2 family court judges added)
        76   Total

1979   5   Supreme court
        5   Court of appeal judges (court of appeals created
            but declared illegal)
        31   Circuit judges (6 "at large" circuit judges added)
        46   Family court judges
        87   Total

1983 5   Supreme court
      6   Court of appeal judges
      31 Circuit court judges
      46 Family court judges
      88 Total

1990 5   Supreme court
      6   Court of appeal judges
      40 Circuit judges (5 resident and 4 "at large" judges added)
      46 Family court judges
      97 Total

1995 5   Supreme court
      9   Court of appeals (3 judges of court of appeals added)
      46 Circuit judges (3 circuit judges added)
      51 Family court judges (3 family court judges added)
      111 Total

All judges are busy and the chief justice has sought additional judges to cope with an over-abundance of cases filed in all courts every year.

49 Wofford College and the Law

Wofford College made history by inviting the South Carolina Bar to hold a continuing legal education seminar on the campus in September 2004. The seminar was well attended. Among those in attendance were William B. Traxler and Karen G. Williams, judges of the Fourth Circuit Court of Appeals. Jean Toal, chief justice of South Carolina, and William Wilkins Jr. of the U.S. Circuit Court of Appeals moderated segments of the seminar.

For many years, Wofford alumni have bragged about the fact that so many of its graduates had come to serve as attorneys and as judges for the various courts. At the time of the seminar, there were 14,366 living alumni of the school. Of this number, 683 were licensed attorneys. This number includes practitioners in small and large firms, sole practitioners, corporate counsel, trust officers, CEOs and other business executives, real estate developers and educators. The 683 alumni attorneys are spread among 26 states of the union.

At the present time, 24 graduates of Wofford are serving as judges at some level throughout the country. Clyde H. Hamilton and Dennis W. Shedd are members of the U.S. Court of Appeals, which sits in Richmond, Virginia. Three members of the Supreme Court of South Carolina are graduates of Wofford College, namely John H. Waller Jr., E.C. Burnett III and Costa M. Pleicones. Each of these three, sometimes referred to as the Wofford Mafia, has been awarded honorary doctorate degrees.

Henry Floyd is a U.S. District Court judge, O. Eugene Powell Jr. is a U.S. Administrative Law judge and Robert H. Hodges Jr. serves on the U.S. Court of Federal Claims. Bruce Williams serves on the S.C. Court of Appeals. Five graduates are presently serving as judges of the S.C. Circuit Court. They are James E. Brogdon Jr., Perry M. Buckner, J. Mark Hayes, D. Gary Hill and William Keesley.

Five graduates of Wofford serve as members of the S.C. Family Courts. They are H. Thomas Abbott III, Roger E. Henderson, Alvin D. Johnson, Marion D. Myers and R. Wright Turbeville.

Additionally, other graduates are serving in a judicial capacity outside of South Carolina. They are Harold C. Arnold (county court judge in Duval County, Florida), N.B. Barefoot Jr. (district court judge in North Carolina), D. Lynn Cobb (general sessions court judge in Tennessee), and Neal W. Dickert (superior court judge in Florida).

In 1985, Wofford boasted that three of its graduates simultaneously held offices of high honor. They were Bruce Littlejohn, chief justice of the Supreme Court of South Carolina; Jacob Jennings, president of the S.C. Bar; and Dan McLeod, state attorney general. Truly, Wofford has made a great contribution to the bench and bar, and to the administration of justice.

50 Technology Arrives

Today, the work of courthouse employees in South Carolina is vastly different from the way business was carried on in 1930. Reference has been made to the many changes in and about the judiciary. The clerk of court performs many services, one of which is to be of assistance to the presiding judges and to record the judge's official documents. In the 1930s, judges were only half-employed. The clerk of court in Spartanburg had three employees who collected fees, fines and recorded judgments. Today he has 38 and each has a computer.

Many of the counties did not have a Register Mesne Conveyance (RMC) Office. A few of the large counties had taken the recordation of deeds and mortgages from the office of the clerk of court and put them in the RMC office. Some of the counties still require the clerk of court to perform the additional chores of recording deeds and mortgages. In the Office of the RMC, deeds and mortgages formerly were recorded with what we referred to as a "book typewriter." The documents were typed into a large permanent book-like binder. To copy the instruments, an employee in the RMC office would put the book in the glorified typewriter and proceed to copy the deed and/or mortgage. This system required the RMC to proofread what the typist had written. It was not until about 1942 that photocopying of deeds and mortgages came into vogue. Photocopying has now been replaced by microfilm.

The computer has come to play an important part in the work of the judge, the clerk of court and lawyer. Chief Justice Jean H. Toal has displayed a great deal of leadership in requiring all judges to have a laptop computer. Gone are the days when the judge had to hatch his own charge to the jury. He or she can, sitting at the bench, pull up a charge that has been approved. In addition, when a case is cited, he or she can pull up cases decided by the Supreme Court of South Carolina, the S.C. Court of Appeals and many other courts.

The day of technology has arrived in the judicial and legal world. It is difficult to find a manual typewriter in a modern-day courthouse or even in a lawyer's office. Gone are the days when a lawyer could practice law with a yellow pad and a pencil. Today he needs an electric typewriter and/or a word processor, a computer, fax machine and copier. In the meantime, the need for books has been minimized. Many lawyers and judges now, in lieu of buying books, merely use the computer.

51 The Future

I predict there will be as many changes in the administration of justice over the next 50 years as we have observed in the past 50 years. Since 1919, our court system has grown from 14 circuit court judges to 46. In 1930, the 14 were not truly busy. The 46 are now overworked;

they never get caught up. During this time we have created 51 family court judgeships.

I wish I could predict a need for fewer courts and fewer judges in the future. The need for more judges and more courts is more likely. It seems that increasingly it is difficult for people to get along and courts are needed to settle disputes. This applies to people in all human relationships – parent and child, teachers and students, vendor and vendee, capital and labor, doctor and patient – and one can carry this on through all relationships in society.

Recently, I was asked why so many causes of action are being filed. I replied, "Maybe it's because so many people ought to be sued." So long as people are inclined to cheat, lie, steal, fail to perform their duty, fail to respect the rights of others and refuse to pay a note at the bank, the work of the courts will increase.

In the last 74 years, bar membership has grown from about 800 to about 10,000. The 10,000 are busier than the 800 were. It is not too early for the bench and bar to begin planning for the increased chores that are soon to be coming our way.

In preparing for the future, we must realize that the need for government and courts will grow. Politicians assert that they are in favor of smaller government and fewer taxes. The growth of government since 1930 is reflected in the size of *The South Carolina Code*. The Code of 1932 consumed about 16 inches on the lawyer's shelf. Today, the code covers about 10 feet on the lawyer's shelf. While advocating smaller government, politicians are consistently passing new laws. Congress is in session most of the year passing laws. The legislatures of most states are in session every year passing laws. County governments and municipalities are constantly passing laws. It is not easy to find which laws should be repealed.

The court system has grown from 19 members in the supreme court and of the circuit courts combined, to more than 100 members of the supreme court, the court of appeals, the circuit courts and the family courts combined. More than 300 magistrates serve South Carolina.

In 1932, the S.C. Legislature appropriated $219,000 for the judicial department. Included in this figure were appropriations for five members of the supreme court and 14 members of the circuit court. They were paid approximately $5,000 per year each.

The total appropriated for the year 2000 was in the neighborhood of $40 million. All of the courts in South Carolina currently functioning are needed and no one advocates the abolition of any of the judgeships. On the other hand, within the foreseeable future, additional judges will be needed and elected.

APPENDIX 1

Supreme Court of South Carolina as of 2004

Jean H. Toal, C.J.
James Edward Moore
John Henry Waller Jr.
E.C. Burnett III
Costa M. Pleicones

APPENDIX 2

South Carolina Court of Appeals as of 2004

Kaye Gorenflo Hearn, C.J.
C. Tolbert Goolsby Jr.
H. Samuel Stilwell
Thomas E. Huff
Ralph King Anderson Jr.
Donald W. "Don" Beatty
John Williamson Kittredge
William L. Howard
* Carol Connor
H. Bruce Williams

*Deceased

APPENDIX 3

Circuit Court Judges as of 2004

Lee S. Alford
James R. Barber III
J. Michael Baxley
John L. Breeden Jr.
James E. Brogdon Jr.
Perry M. Buckner
Paul M. Burch
J. Derham Cole
G. Thomas Cooper Jr.
Thomas W. Cooper Jr.
Roger L. Couch
R. Markley Dennis Jr.
Doyet A. Early III
John C. Few
Kenneth G. Goode
Diane S. Goodstein
Jackson V. Gregory
B. Hicks Harwell Jr.
J. Mark Hayes II
John C. Hayes III
D. Garrison Hill
Deadra L. Jefferson
Steven H. John
James W. Johnson Jr.

William P. Keesley
J. Ernest Kinard Jr.
Howard P. King
Alison R. Lee
Reginald I. Lloyd
James E. Lockemy
Alexander S. Macauley
J. Cordell Maddox Jr.
L. Casey Manning
Edward J. Miller
John M. Milling
Clifton B. Newman
Julius C. Nicholson Jr.
Larry R. Patterson
Rodney A. Peeples
Daniel F. Pieper
Wyatt T. Saunders
Paul E. Short
Paula H. Thomas
G. Edward Welmaker
*Marc H. Westbrook
James C. Williams Jr.
Roger M. Young

*Deceased

APPENDIX 4

Family Court Judges as of 2004

Haskell T. Abbott III
Kellum W. Allen
Georgia V. Anderson
Robert S. Armstrong
Stephen S. Bartlett
Hugh E. Bonnoitt Jr.
Judy C. Bridges
Timothy L. Brown
Walter B. Brown Jr.
Wesley L. Brown
Mary E. Buchan
Timothy M. Cain
Wylie H. Caldwell Jr.
Richard W. Chewning III
Wayne M. Creech
Tommy B. Edwards
Jane Dowling Fender
James F. Fraley Jr.
Dale M. Gable
Paul W. Garfinkel
Jocelyn C. Ginsburg
Brooks L. Goldsmith
Robert E. Guess
Roger E. Henderson
Rolly W. Jacobs
Robert N. Jenkins Sr.
Alvin D. Johnson

R. Kinard Johnson Jr.
Anne Gue Jones
Lisa A. Kinon
Barry W. Knobel
Aphrodite K. Konduros
Jack A. Landis
George M. McFaddin Jr.
Joseph W. McGowan III
Nancy C. McLin
Arthur E. Morehead III
J.L. Murdock Jr.
Marion D. Myers
Peter R. Nuessle
Leslie K. Riddle
John M. Rucker
C. David Sawyer Jr.
Frances P. Segars-Andrews
Gerald C. Smoak Jr.
James A. Spruill III
Donna S. Strom
Billy A. Tunstall Jr.
Ralston W. Turbeville
Jerry D. Vinson Jr.
Henry T. Woods
William J. Wylie Jr.
W. Jeffery Young

APPENDIX 5

Administrative Law Judges as of 2004

Marvin F. Kittrell, C.J.
H. Dukes Scott
Carolyn C. Matthews
John D. Geathers
Ray N. Stevens
Ralph K. Anderson III

INDEX